USAF Strategic Bomber Operations

B-52H, B-1B and B-2A
Operation Allied Force
Balkans 1999

Hugh Shrakin

USAF Strategic Bomber Operations

B-52H, B-1B and B-2A
Operation Allied Force
Balkans 1999

© Hugh Shrakin 2015

Published by Centurion Publishing
United Kingdom

ISBN 10: 1-903630-41-X
ISBN 13: 978-1-903630-41-9

This volume first published in 2015

The Author is identified as the copyright holder of this work under sections 77 and 78 of the Copyright Designs and Patents Act 1988

Cover design © Centurion Publishing & Createspace

Page layout, concept and design © Centurion Publishing

The traditional start of chapter on the recto side only has been intentionally disregarded; chapters starting on either the recto or verso side as required in the interests of the environment

All rights reserved. No part of this publication may be reproduced, stored in a retrieval system, transmitted in any form, or by any means, electronic, mechanical or photocopied, recorded or otherwise, without the written permission of the Publisher

The Publisher and Author would like to thank all organisations and services for their assistance and contributions in the preparation of this volume

USAF Strategic Bomber Operations

B-52H, B-1B and B-2A
Operation Allied Force
Balkans 1999

Contents

Introduction	4
Chapter 1: The USAF Bomber Trio	5
Chapter 2: Operation Allied Force	46
Appendices	94
Glossary	95

Introduction

In spring 1999 the NATO Alliance launched Operation Allied Force - a sustained 79 day bombing campaign against Serbia. This campaign saw the USAF employ all three types of strategic bombers in its inventory, the B-52H, B-1B and B-2A, with a diversity of guided and unguided ordnance being employed.

The purpose of this volume is to describe the operational use of the triad of USAF strategic bombers employed against Serbia. It is not the remit of this volume to discuss the rights and wrongs of the campaign, or give an in depth political or military analysis, although there will, of course, be occasions when politics and ethics emerge in the narration of events. The volume also briefly describes the strategic bomber trio, B-52H, B-1B and B-2A, employed in the campaign, as well as the ordnance dropped, and narrates the strategic bomber roadway from the United States extraction from the Vietnam War in 1973 to the inventory in 1999. Appendices detail the bombers that took part in the operation and the weapons employed.

All facts and figures used in the preparation of this volume have come from official source documentation such as the USAF and NATO.

Chapter 1

The USAF Strategic Bomber Trio

The B-1B overcame early operational problems to mature into a potent weapon system. USAF

In the years following the United States withdrawal from the Vietnam War in 1973, and the end to the bombing of Cambodia and Laos in August 1973, the USAF SAC (Strategic Air Command) Boeing B-52 Stratofortress fleet dropped the conventional bombing role and concentrated completely on the nuclear strike mission. Older models of the B-52 were retired, including the B-52D, which had born the lion's share of conventional bombing missions in South East Asia. By the mid-1980's only the short tailed B-52G/H models remained in service.

By 1990, SAC operated B-52G, B-52H, Rockwell (Boeing) B-1B and General Dynamics FB-111A bombers in 16 Bomb Wings. Only the B-52G's were tasked with a conventional bombing role; the B-52H and B-1B being assigned a nuclear role. The conventional role for the B-52G had re-commenced in 1988, with a number of aircraft tasked to fly conventional bombing and anti-ship strike missions armed with McDonnell Douglas AGM-84 Harpoon missiles for the latter.

In 1999, the USAF bomber trio consisted of the B-52H, farthest from camera, B-1B, centre, and the B-2A. USAF

When it entered service in the mid-1980's the Rockwell B-1B was tasked with the nuclear strike role armed with B61 and B83 gravity nuclear bombs. USAF

By late 1990, SAC operated 157 of 193 B-52G's produced. Ninety-eight of these had been converted to carry the Boeing AGM-86B ALCM (Air Launched Cruise Missile), armed with the W-80 nuclear warhead. SAC also operated 94 of 102 B-52H's built, which were tasked with a standoff nuclear strike role armed with the AGM-86B. This weapon could be released from stand-off ranges in excess of 1,000 miles, negating the need for the cumbersome bomber to penetrate heavily defended Soviet airspace.

Concerns about the B-52's ability to successfully penetrate heavily defended Soviet airspace saw the variable-geometry B-1B procured as SAC's primary penetrator. This large aircraft, which could fly at speeds up to Mach 1.2, was designed with reduced radar signature as a design driver. While not being a dedicated 'stealth' driven aircraft design, the B-1B has a RCS (Radar Cross Section) only about one quarter that of the B-52. The USAF received 100 B-1B's 97 of which remained in the inventory in 1990. Two of these aircraft were assigned to on-going development and testing with 95 aircraft assigned to 4 BW (Bomb Wings) based at Dyess AFB, Texas, Ellsworth AFB, South Dakota, Grand Forks AFB, North Dakota and McConnell AFB, Kansas.

The Northrop Grumman B-2A 'stealth' bomber was still under development in the late 1980's when the SAC returned to the conventional bombing role. The first B-2A, 82-1066, is formally unveiled in 1989. US DoD

bombers in 2 Bomb Wings. The primary role of the FB-111A was to attack Soviet Air Defence sites ahead of SAC heavy bomber packages. The primary weapon for this mission was the Boeing AGM-69 SRAM (Short-Range Attack Missile), which had a 200-KT W-69 nuclear warhead. The FB-111A could also carry the B28/61 gravity nuclear bombs.

In the early 1990's, the FB-111A was transferred to TAC (Tactical Air Command) and re-designated F-111G, then finally retired from USAF service along with TAC's F-111E/F's. The B-52G was completely retired by the end of 1994. The B-1B force lost the nuclear role, and, together with the B-52H, took on the conventional role. The B-52H retained the nuclear strike mission as its primary role, although the force would be employed in conventional roles throughout the 1990's and into the 21st Century.

The planned new bomber for the USAF, the Northrop B-2A, developed under the ATB (Advanced Tactical Bomber) program, eventually entered service in December 1993. The B-2A is a 'stealth' driven design, which traded flight performance such as supersonic speed capability for reduced visibility to radar, acoustic and infrared sensors.

Prior to the 1988 re-allocation of a conventional bombing role to some B-52G's, it had been fifteen years since USAF SAC bombers had dropped conventional bombs in anger. Top: This pair of B-52D bombers are dropping M117 750-lb. bombs on targets in south East Asia during the Vietnam War. The B-52D 'Big Belly' conversion allowed this model to carry more ordnance than any other B-52 model. Above: A pair of B-52D's en-route to the target area during the south East Asia conflicts. Boeing

In 1990, SAC still operated around 48 General Dynamics FB-111A variable-geometry strike

SAC operated the FB-111A until the early 1990's. This small supersonic bomber was tasked with attacking Soviet air defence systems with AGM-69 SRAM nuclear missiles to clear a path for the larger B-52 attacking strategic targets. USAF

A B-1B lands at a UK airbase in September 1996. At this time the B-1B's conventional role remained more or less a high-tech bomb truck armed with MK 80 series 'iron' bombs. H Harkins

With the thawing of East/West relations SAC bombers were stood-down from nuclear alert status on 27 September 1991. SAC itself was disbanded on 1 June 1992, its bomber assets combining with the assets of TAC to form ACC (Air Combat Command). At the same time SAC's tanker force was transferred to AMC (Air Mobility Command).

Cuts to the ACC bomber force during the 1990's and early 2000's saw the force further streamlined as the B-2A came on strength and new precision guided and near precision guided weapons were introduced to the inventory of all three active bomber types. By the early 2000's ACC's bomber force comprised five Bomb Wings operating three bomber types at five CONUS (Continental United States) bases. The 2nd BW, Barksdale AFB, Louisiana and the 5th BW, Minot AFB, North Dakota, operated the B-52H, the 7th BW, Dyess AFB, Texas and 28th BW, Ellsworth AFB, South Dakota, both operated the B-1B and the 509th BW, Whiteman AFB, Missouri, operated the B-2A.

Boeing B-52 Stratofortress

Despite entering service with SAC in June 1955, the B-52, in 1990, three and a half decades later, remained the primary SAC long-range strategic bomber, albeit in more recent models, which had undergone continuous updates.

As well as the AGM-86B ALCM, the B-52H was also armed with the AGM-129 Advanced Cruise Missile, which was a stealthy cruise missile, armed with a nuclear warhead, developed, initially, as a successor to the ALCM. Boeing

The Boeing XB-52 (above) and the YB-52 models had the tandem cockpit arrangement, dropped in the production variants. Boeing

The Stratofortress, known affectionately as the BUFF (Big Ugly Fat Fella, or Fucker, depending on the colourfulness of the narrators language), emerged as a result of the search for a replacement for the Convair B-36 Peacemaker in SAC service. Boeing designers originally submitted their model 464-35 with turboprop engines, but were requested to amend the basic design to incorporate jet engines, namely the JT3, which received the military designation J57. Four days later, Boeing submitted their new proposal which was met with enthusiasm by the USAF, which promptly issued a contract order for a prototype XB-52 and an YB-52 test airframe, both of which were appropriated with FY (Fiscal Year) 1949 funds.

Like the B-36 before it, the B-52 was a large aircraft, with a span of 59.39-m (185-ft), and a length of 47.727-m (156-ft 7-in). The height of the early models was 14.724-m (48-ft 3.8-in), with an empty weight of just under 200,000-lb. and a maximum take-off weight of over 400,000-lb. Power was supplied by eight Pratt & Whitney (J57-P-29) turbojet engines, housed in four tandem pods below the wings; each engine developing 5489-kg (12,100-lb) thrust.

The prototype XB-52 was rolled out on the night of 29 November 1951. The secrecy surrounding the program at this time saw the huge bomber covered by massive white sheets. The second aircraft, the YB-52, was rolled out the following March and conducted its first flight on 15 April 1952, ahead of the XB-52 which conducted its maiden flight on 2 October that year.

With upwards of 500 aircraft required by the USAF, it was hoped that a development batch of 13 aircraft would be purchased to conduct a lengthy test program. However as the USAF wanted to get the new bomber into service as quickly as possible it was decided that a batch of three B-52As would be purchased from the FY 1952 defence budget to be used in the development program. The first B-52A was rolled out in March 1954 and conducted its maiden flight on 5 August that year.

The prototype B-52A is seen on its first flight on 5 August 1954. Boeing

Top: Ten aircraft designated B-52B were ordered in 1953. Above: A total of 35 B-52C's were built. This B-52C is seen during a flight in the 1950's. USAF

A further ten aircraft designated B-52B were ordered in 1953, although these aircraft were re-designated RB-52B as they were intended as duel role reconnaissance/bomber aircraft. For the reconnaissance role they were equipped with a photographic capsule housed in the bomb bay. A further 21 B-52Bs were ordered in 1953, these aircraft being purely intended for the bomber role with no reconnaissance capability.

The first operational unit to receive the B-52 was the 93rd Bomb Wing at Castle AFB, California, which received its first aircraft toward the end of June 1955.

The B-52B/RB-52B was followed on the production line by the B-52C, ten of which were ordered in 1953, followed by another 25 ordered in 1954. Among the improvements featured in the B-52C was a new navigation bombing system. In 1955/56, 170 B-52Ds were ordered, this being the first large-scale production variant. From 1956, the B-52D's were followed by 100 B-52E's, these introducing a more capable navigation bombing system developed by IBM, resulting in a redesigned cockpit. The B-52E was followed by 89 B-52F's, which introduced the up-rated J57 water injected engines.

The B-52D was the first large-scale production variant. Top: The first flight of the first Wichita, Kansas built B-52D in 1956. Boeing Centre: The B-52D bore the brunt of the USAF strategic bomber effort in the conflicts in South East Asia in the 1960's and early 1970's. The Big Belly modifications enabled the 'D' to haul more bombs than any other variant. Above: Like a scene from the movie Dr Strangelove, variant aside, a B-52E is refuelled by a Boeing KC-135A Stratotanker. B-52 operations were synonymous with the KC-135A, which gave the B-52 its global strike capability. USAF

The B-52F, like the B-52D and B-52G, was committed to SAC's bombing campaigns over SEA. The B-52F's quad 0.5-in machine gun tail armament was typical of all models except the B-52H, which was armed with a 20 mm Vulcan cannon, the gun position being manned on all variants except the B-52G/H. USAF

A further 21 B-52Fs were cancelled, the order being diverted to B-52G production, 193 of which were manufactured. The B-52G was designed to be capable of carrying the North American GAM-77 (AGM-28) Hound Dog inertial-guidance stand-off nuclear missile as well as the McDonnell Douglas ADM-20 Quail decoy. Major changes to the design were introduced with the B-52G, the most obvious external change being the short tail of only 12.40-m (40-ft 8-in) compared with the 14.724-m of the earlier variants. Internally the changes were considerable, and included a new integral-tank wing increasing the internal fuel capacity to 46,576 US gal. (176309 litres), allowing the large 3,000 US gal wing mounted droppable external tanks to be replaced by smaller 700 US gal. (2650 litre) fixed under wing tanks. The manned tail gun position of the earlier models was replaced by a gunners position in the main crew compartment. The gunner operated the guns, four 0.50 in (12.7 mm) machine guns, by remote control via the AN/ASG-15 fire control system. The airframe was strengthened, allowing maximum take-off weight to be increased to 221357-kg (488,000-lb.).

Following the B-52G was the further improved B-52H, 102 of which were ordered during 1960-61 and delivered during 1961/62. The B-52H retained the short tail introduced on the B-52G, but introduced a host of improvements, most significant of which was the replacement of the J57 jet engines with 8 Pratt & Whitney TF33-P-3 turbofan engines rated at 75.65-kN (17,000-lb.) for take-off. The more powerful engines allowed an increase in take-off weight, higher operating ceiling and reduced cabin noise, and had a much lower fuel burn with the knock-on effect of increasing range over previous models. Water-methanol boosting was provided for take-off and a 1,200 US gal. (4542 litre) saddle tank was located behind the crew compartment.

The penultimate B-52 variant was the B-52G, which introduced a number of improvements over earlier generation B-52's. Externally the B-52G could easily be distinguished from earlier variants by the shorter tail. The B-52G, however, retained many features common to earlier variants such as the J57 turbojet engines and the quad rear mounted gun defensive armament. The latter relinquished the rear turret gunner position in favour of a gunner's position in the forward crew compartment; the guns being fired by remote control. US DoD

There have been a number of proposals to re-engine the B-52H to extend service life and reduce maintenance and operating costs. In 1996, Boeing proposed to re-engine up to 94 B-52H's with the Rolls Royce RB.211-535E4-B turbofan used in civil airliners. However, all plans to re-engine the aircraft fell by the wayside.

The remotely operated tail gun position was retained although the armament was changed from the four machine guns to a single T-171 (M-61A1) six-barrel 20-mm Vulcan cannon. Like the preceding B-52G, the B-52H was capable of carrying the Quail decoy as well as the Hound Dog missile but was also designed with carriage of the GAM-87A Skybolt ALBM (Air Launched Ballistic Missile) in mind. The Skybolt project was eventually cancelled.

The first B-52H was delivered on 30 September 1960 and the last was accepted on 26 October 1962, bringing to an end a production run which spanned 744 B-52's of all variants.

Top right: A B-52G launches an AGM-109 Tomahawk cruise missile during trials with the weapon in the early 1980's. US DoD **Above: A B-52H Rivet Ace 1 aircraft carrying AGM-69 SRAM missiles in 1975.** USAF

The B-52H fleet eventually adopted a drab one tone green camouflage scheme as worn by 61-1031 in September 2004. H Harkins

With the changing operational environment the B-52 had to undergo improvements to remain a viable strike platform. In 1972, the USAF began equipping most of its B-52 fleet with an electronic suite to allow it to operate at low level in adverse weather day and night. Known as the Electro-optical Viewing System, it incorporates silicide platinum FLIR (Forward Looking Infrared) and high resolution LLLTV (Low Light Level Television) sensors which provide images of the view ahead of the aircraft on screens in the cockpit, which, combined with the terrain-avoidance radar, enables the aircraft to accurately navigate and fly at low level without outside visibility due to either bad weather, night conditions, or if the nuclear window blinds are down. As well as flight-safety, these sensors also assist with targeting and damage assessment. In 1976, the Rivet Ace program was introduced, updating the aircrafts ECM (Electronic Countermeasures) suite.

Pilots were equipped with NVG (Night Vision Goggles), enhancing night vision during flight, increasing aircraft safety, terrain and other close proximity aircraft being more easily visually acquired during a lights out environment.

The most significant change between the B-52G and the B-52H was the latter's adoption of TF33 turbofan engines to replace the J57's. H Harkins

Left from top to bottom: In the 1990's, the lack of any serious air threat for scenarios envisioned for the aircraft, combined with a drive to reduce operating costs, saw the B-52H lose its 20-mm tail cannon defensive armament; the cannon housing being faired over (top). The B-52H is equipped with a large fuselage weapons bay (centre top), which can carry 27 x 750-lb. bombs. The wings are fitted with Heavy Stores Adaptor Beams (centre bottom) allowing the carriage of large weapons like the AGM-142A. The crew of the B-52H are all housed in the forward section of the aircraft (bottom). Top right: From the 1970's, the B-52H underwent progressive updates allowing it to continue in service into the 21st Century. The additional sensors produced a number of lumps and bumps, particularly at the front of the aircraft. Author

From the mid to late 1970's, the B-52H regularly practiced for the low-level strike role armed with nuclear and later conventional weapons. Operational B-52H missions are typically flown at medium to high altitudes. USAF

The current B-52H is well equipped to handle threats from hostile radar systems. The ECM equipment suite includes an ALT-28 jammer housed in a fairing on top of the nose, an ALQ-172 deception jammer located just forward of the gun control radar, the RWR (Radar Warning Receiver) antennas are located in the tail cone and on blisters on both sides of the vertical fin, and the forward and rear under fuselage sections are home to clusters of aerials for the ALQ-155 system.

Located behind the huge upward hinging nose is the Norden APQ-156 multi-mode radar, which incorporates SAR (Synthetic Aperture Radar) technology. The principal function of the radar is targeting. An ASG-15 gun laying radar was located in the tail of the aircraft, which directed fire from the rear turret 20-mm Vulcan cannon until the defensive armament system was removed in the early 1990's.

Since the late 1980's, the B-52H has been undergoing on-going rolling modifications which have seen many improvements including the incorporation of a GPS (Global Positioning System), HSAB (Heavy Stores Adaptor Beam) to allow the carriage of 2,000-lb MK84 bombs externally, and aircraft/weapons interfaces allowing the aircraft to be integrated with new advanced weapons like the Boeing GBU-31 JDAM (Joint Direct Attack Munitions).

The B-52H can carry a large variety of conventional and nuclear weapons. In the conventional role up to 27 MK 84 907-kg (2,000-lb) bombs can be carried internally with a further eighteen carried externally, nine on each of two inboard wing pylons with stub pylons and heavy stores adapter beam. Alternatively 27 x 340-kg (750-lb) M117 or MK83 454-kg (1000-lb) bombs can be accommodated internally with a further 12 on each inboard under wing pylon on multiple ejector racks. The 500-lb MK82 LDGP (Low Drag General-Purpose) bomb can also be carried internally along with another 24 carried externally.

The B-52H could not carry as much ordnance as earlier variants like the B-52D. However, the 'H', which increasingly took on the conventional bombing role following the retirement of the B-52G, could still carry an impressive load of up to 51 750-lb bombs in the internal weapons bay and on the under wing stations. This B-52H is dropping MK82 500 lb. retarded bombs. USAF

The AGM-142A Have Nap TV-guided missile provides an 80-km (50 mile) stand-off capability. This weapon, which is a development of the Israeli Rafael Popeye missile, has an 896-kg (1,975-lb.) high explosive warhead. The conventionally armed AGM-86C CALCM (Conventional Air Launched Cruise Missile) allows targets at considerably longer range to be attacked.

The new generation of 'J' weapons mentioned above can be carried, as can other PGM's such as LGB (Laser Guided Bombs) and newer generation cluster munitions like the WCMD (Wind Corrected Munitions Dispenser and SFW (Sensor Fused Weapon) These new weapon options have revolutionised the capabilities of the venerable B-52, in theory allowing dozens of targets to be accurately struck on a single sortie.

The huge weight of the B-52 is supported on the ground by four twin-wheel bogies, which retract into the fuselage. H Harkins

A B-1B is powered into the sky by its four General Electric F101-GE-102 afterburning turbofan engines, each rated at 30,000-lb thrust with afterburner. H Harkins

The B-52H has an un-refuelled combat range in excess of 14080-km (8,800 miles) according to USAF figures. One or multiple in-flight refuelling allow mission to be increased with flight duration dictated by crew endurance.

While the USAF operates only the B-52H, NASA (National Aeronautics and Space Administration), until recently, operated B-52B 52-0008 designated NB-52B, which was the oldest B-52 still flying until retired in 2004. This aircraft was used as the air drop mother ship for a number of NASA 'X' programs until replaced by a loaned USAF B-52H transferred to NASA.

The B-52 has been extensively employed on operational missions since June 1965 when B-52Fs from the 7th and 320th Bomb Wings flew Arc Light missions over South Vietnam from Anderson AFB, Guam. The B-52D deployed to Guam in April 1966, replacing the B-52Fs in South East Asia. The 'D' model remained for the remainder of the Vietnam War and in 1972 was joined by the short tailed B-52G. B-52s also operated from Okinawa and Thailand. B-52G's were employed during the 1991 Gulf war and the B-52H flew strike missions against Iraq in 1996 and 1998.

Boeing B-52H Stratofortress
Type: strategic bomber
Power plant: Eight Pratt & Whitney TF33-P-3/103 non-afterburning turbofan engines each rated at 75.63-kN (17,000-lb)
Wingspan: 56.4-m (185-ft)
Wing area: 371.6-m2 (4,000 sq. ft.)
Length: 48.5-m (159-ft 4-in
Height: 12.4-m (40-ft 8-in)
Wheelbase: 15.48-m (50-ft 3-in)
Wheel track: 2.51-m (8-ft 3-in)
Weights: Approximately 83250-kg (185,000-lb.) empty and 219600-kg (488,000-lb.) maximum take off
Fuel: Internal fuel 135821-kg (299,434-lb.); external fuel 4134-kg (9,114-lb.) in two 700-US gal (2650 litre) under wing fuel tanks
Maximum level speed: Mach 0.86 (650-mph)
Ceiling: 15151.5-m (50,000-ft)
Un-refuelled range: 8,800 miles (7,652-nm)
Armament: USAF figures state that approximately 31500-kg (70,000-lb) of mixed ordnance may be carried

This head-on view of a B-1B of the 9th BS, over the Bearing Sea, shows the sheer bulk of the aircraft's fuselage, designed to accommodate three large internal weapon bays. USAF

Boeing (Rockwell) B-1B Lancer

The Boeing (Rockwell) B-1B is a developed variant of the Rockwell B-1A strategic bomber, which was developed in the 1970's as a planned successor to the Boeing B-52. The B-1A was designed as a supersonic variable-geometry (swing-wing) strategic bomber capable of speeds of Mach 2.2 at medium and high altitudes. Four prototypes were built and flight-tested before the program was cancelled by the Carter administration in 1977.

Although the program had been cancelled flight-testing of the prototypes continued until April 1981. In that year, the Reagan administration resurrected the program under the guise of the B-1B. This variant retained the overall design layout of the B-1A, but introduced a number of changes, which included an additional structure to increase internal payload to 74,000-lb. A new-improved radar was added and the RCS (Radar Cross Section) of the aircraft was reduced by an order of magnitude. This required the engine inlets to be redesigned, requiring a reduction in maximum speed to Mach 1.2.

B-1B defensive avionics are centred on an AN/ALQ-161A Radio Frequency Surveillance Electronic Countermeasures System, which is basically a self-protection jammer. A tail warning system is coupled to a chaff/flare dispenser and an ALE-50 Towed Radar Decoy system.

The primary sensor is the AN/APQ-164 ORS, which was developed from a variant of the Northrop Grumman (Westinghouse) AN/APG-66/68 fighter radar developed for the Lockheed Martin (formerly General Dynamics) F-16A/B. The radar, flight-tested on a B-52 in 1977, was further developed for the B-1B, featuring a single fixed phased-array (electronically scanned) antenna. The radar system features a number of advanced modes including a variety of attack and terrain following modes allowing the large bomber to penetrate enemy air space at ultra-low level if required.

Four B-1A development aircraft were built with serials 74-158, 74-159, 74-160 and 76-174. The prototype conducted its first flight on 23 December 1974, but the program was cancelled on 30 June 1977, by which time 118 flights had been conducted. Top: and upper left: The third B-1A, 74-160. Lower left: An instrumented B-1A during a test flight. Above right: A B-1A in a disruptive camouflage scheme. Above: The last of the prototypes, 76-174, adopted a sand and greenish scheme. USAF

In late 1981 the B-1 program was resurrected under the guise of the B-1B with a number of improvements incorporated. To speed up the program two of the B-1A development aircraft, 74-159 and 76-174, were modified to flight test systems for the B-1B, 74-160 flying in B-1B guise on 23 March 1983, followed by 76-174 on 30 June 1984. The No.2 B-1A, 74-159, is here flying in support of the B-1B program, with appropriate stencilling on the tail. USAF

The first B-1B conducted its maiden flight in October 1984. An early B-1B (top) together with an F-111 chase aircraft in 1985/86. Above: A B-1B takes-off on 25 October 1986. USAF

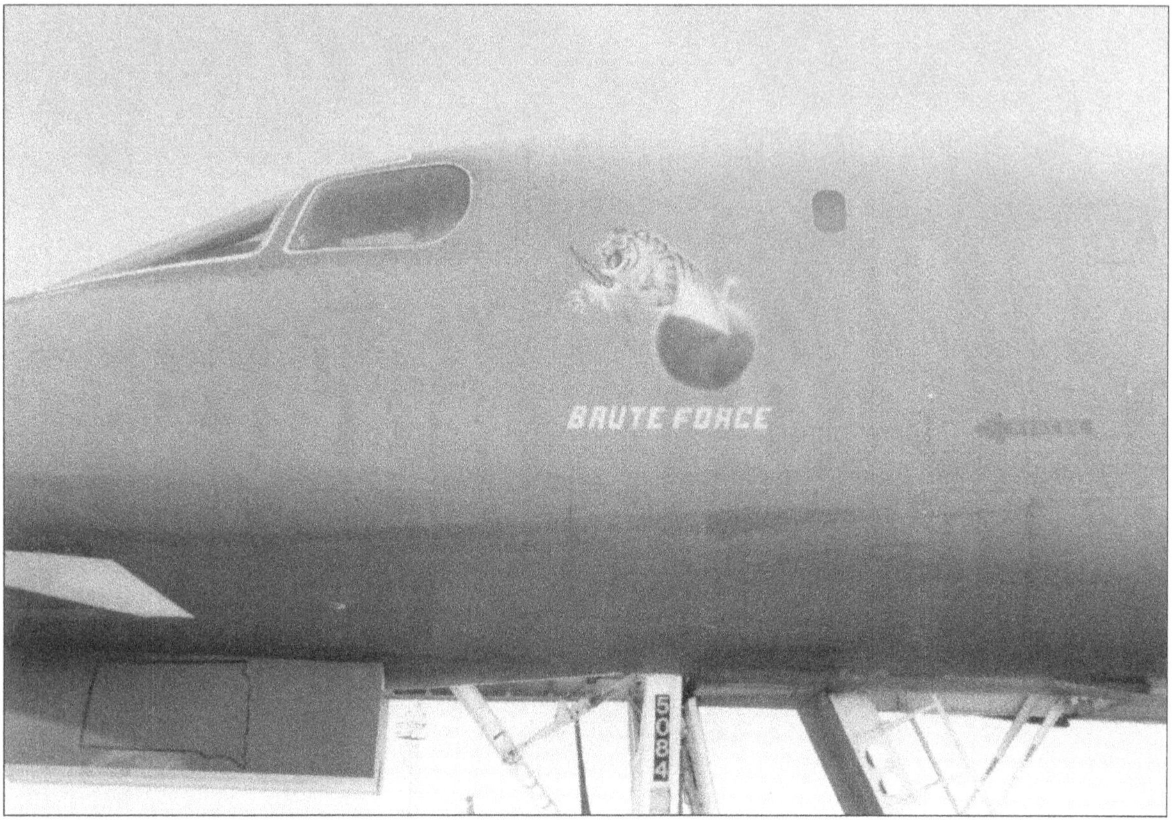
BRUTE FORCE
5084

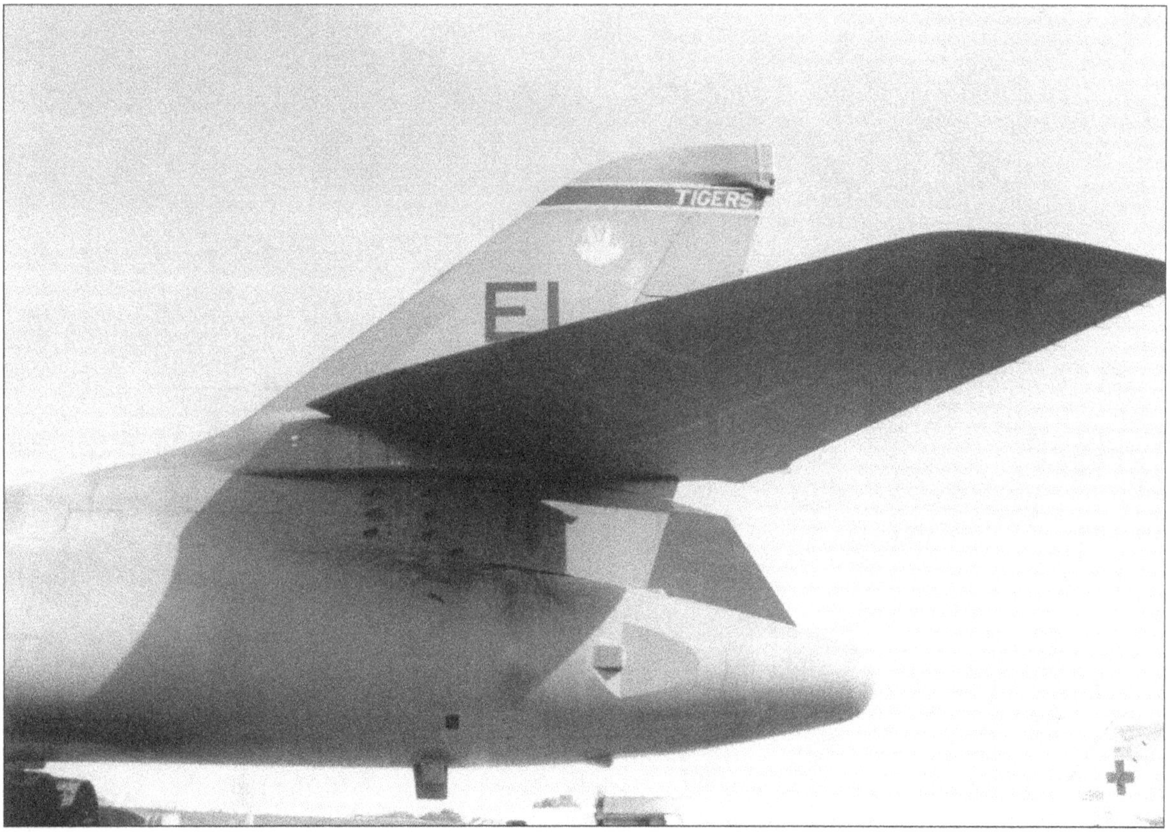
TIGERS
EL

Previous page top: **The forward fuselage of this B-1B is adorned with nose artwork 'Brute Force', which is no exaggeration for the B-1B when used as a bomb truck.** Previous page bottom: **The B-1B is equipped with a sophisticated suite of defensive electronics including the AN/ALQ-161A Tail-Warner mounted in the tail of the aircraft.** This page above: **The 120,000-lb combined thrust of the B-1B's four turbofan engines provides plenty of power for take-off and hauling a large payload to targets thousands of miles distant.** H Harkins

The first B-1B conducted its maiden flight on 18 October 1984, and the first aircraft allocated for USAF service was delivered to Dyess AFB, Texas in June 1985, with IOC (Initial Operational Capability) attained on 1 October 1986. One hundred B-1B's were ordered and the last aircraft was delivered to the USAF on 2 May 1988.

IOC as a nuclear bomber armed with gravity bombs was achieved in FY1987. The CMUP (Conventional Mission Upgrade Program) began in 1993, as retirement of the B-52G was speeding-up. The CMUP would see the B-1B lose its nuclear role as it transitioned to a conventional only mission. The main goals of the CMUP were to increase the B-1B's conventional weapons capability, increase situational awareness and survivability and improve the bombers supportability.

Four F101-GE-102 afterburning turbofan engines, each rated at 30,000-lb thrust with afterburner, power the B-1B. H Harkins

Top: One hundred B-1B's were built supplementing, but not replacing the B-52G/H variants of the Stratofortress. Above: The B-1B equipped the 28th Bomb Wing at Ellsworth AFB, South Dakota. The sleek lines and supersonic flight performance were a far cry from the lumbering B-52, which had never earned a reputation as an attractive aircraft. USAF

Top: A B-1B rolls to its dispersal after landing in 1996. H Harkins **Upper left:** Despite its large size, the sleek design and variable-geometry wings of the B-1B confer excellent handling qualities. Boeing **Lower left:** A B-1B releases a GBU-31 JDAM during trials. USAF **Above:** A B-1B houses a Lockheed Martin AGM-158 JASSM (Joint Air to Surface Stand-off Missile) in the aft weapons bay during trials to clear the weapon for operation from the aircraft. USAF

A B-1B Lancer taxis along the runway at a UK airbase after landing in 1996. A spate of accidents and a primary nuclear role largely precluded B-1B detachments to Europe on the same scale as seen by the older B-52G/H during the 1980's and early 1990's. With the introduction of a conventional bombing role, the Lancer became a much more familiar sight in European Skies. H Harkins

Top: A B-1B in a climb during a test flight in the 1990's. Above: A Dyess AFB based B-1B flies at relatively low-altitude with wings in the swept back position. Boeing

A B-1B with wings in the fully un-swept (forward) position. USAF

Prior to the CMUP, the B-1B could carry only nuclear gravity bombs and MK82 500-lb. conventional bombs. The CMUP was conducted in blocks. The Block B upgrade saw the aircraft receive software upgrades for its defensive systems. The Block C introduced CBU-87/98/97 cluster bomb capability and the Block D introduced upgrades to the communications systems, a GPS navigation system and the capability to carry and release the GBU-31 2,000-lb. JDAM. The Block D IOTE (Initial Operational Test and Evaluation) was conducted at Edwards AFB, California from August to September 1998 with FDE (Force Development Evaluation) commencing at Ellsworth AFB, South Dakota in November 1998. Problems with the UHF/VHF radio system saw the FDE temporarily suspended in early 1999 before being re-started.

The Block E upgrade included computer upgrades giving increased weapon flexibility and supportability and integration of the WCMD (Wind Corrected Munitions Dispenser). In Block F, the defensive avionics suite would be upgraded by integrating a RWR (Radar Warning Receiver), a radio frequency countermeasures system and a fibre-optic Towed Radar Decoy.

B-1B Lancer (USAF figures)
Engines: Four General Electric F101-GE-102 afterburning turbofan engines each rated at 30,000-lb. thrust with afterburner
Length: 44.5-m (146-ft.)
Wingspan: 41.8-m (137-ft.) fully spread (15°), 79-ft. fully swept (67.5°)
Height: 10.4-m (34-ft.)
Weights: Approximately 86183-kg (190,000-lb.) empty and over 216634-kg (470,000-lb.) maximum take-off.
Speed: Mach 1.2 (913-mph) at sea level, Cruising speed around Mach 0.9
Range: Intercontinental, 7.500 miles un-refuelled
Ceiling: Approximately 18288-m (60,000-ft.)
Payload: Variety of ordnance, up to 84 x MK82 500-lb. bombs
Crew: 4 - Aircraft commander, pilot, offensive systems operator and defensive system operator

The B-2A emerged as the end product of the USAF ATB program. Boeing

Northrop Grumman/Boeing B-2A Spirit

While the Reagan administration had resurrected the B-1 program to provide a quick solution to the growing problem of the increasing age of the SAC bomber fleet, the USAF had also embarked upon a program initially known as the ATB (Advanced Tactical Bomber), which was to be designed as a third generation 'stealth' aircraft capable of penetrating heavily defended airspace through a combination of reduced RCS, stealth material coatings and advanced sensors designed for reduced emissions.

The design chosen for the aircraft, which emerged as the Northrop Grumman B-2A, was a flying wing, coming from the Northrop stable, which had designed and flown a number of flying wing designs since the 1940's. The B-2A adopted a revolutionary blending of advanced low-observable technologies into a highly efficient aerodynamic airframe. The heart of the B-2A's stealth capabilities is the low observable technologies which consist of a combination of reduced radar, infrared, acoustic and electromagnetic signatures. The highly efficient tail-less flying wing design also contributes to making the aircraft more difficult to acquire visually compared with its predecessors.

This early artist impression of the ATB was released in the 1980's. US DoD

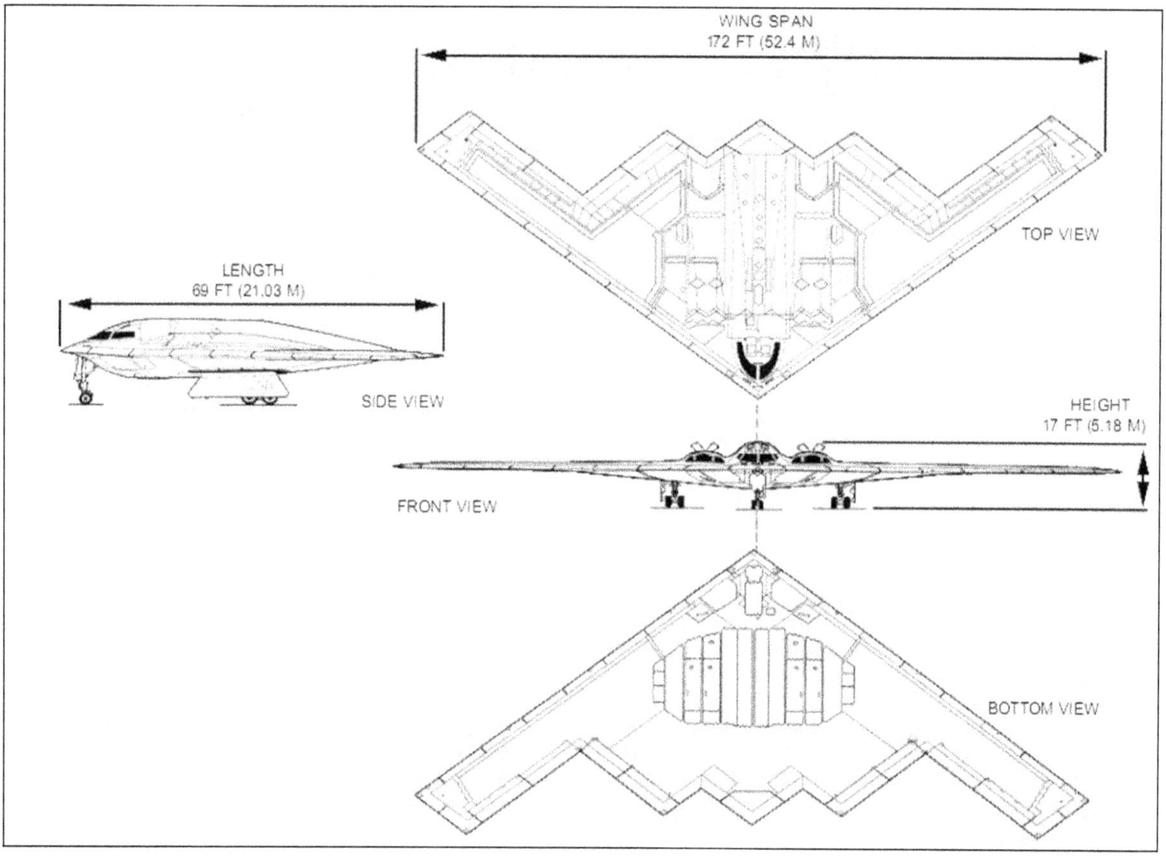

Top: The first B-2A, S/N: 82-1066, during a development flight. **Above:** General arrangement drawing of the B-2A. USAF

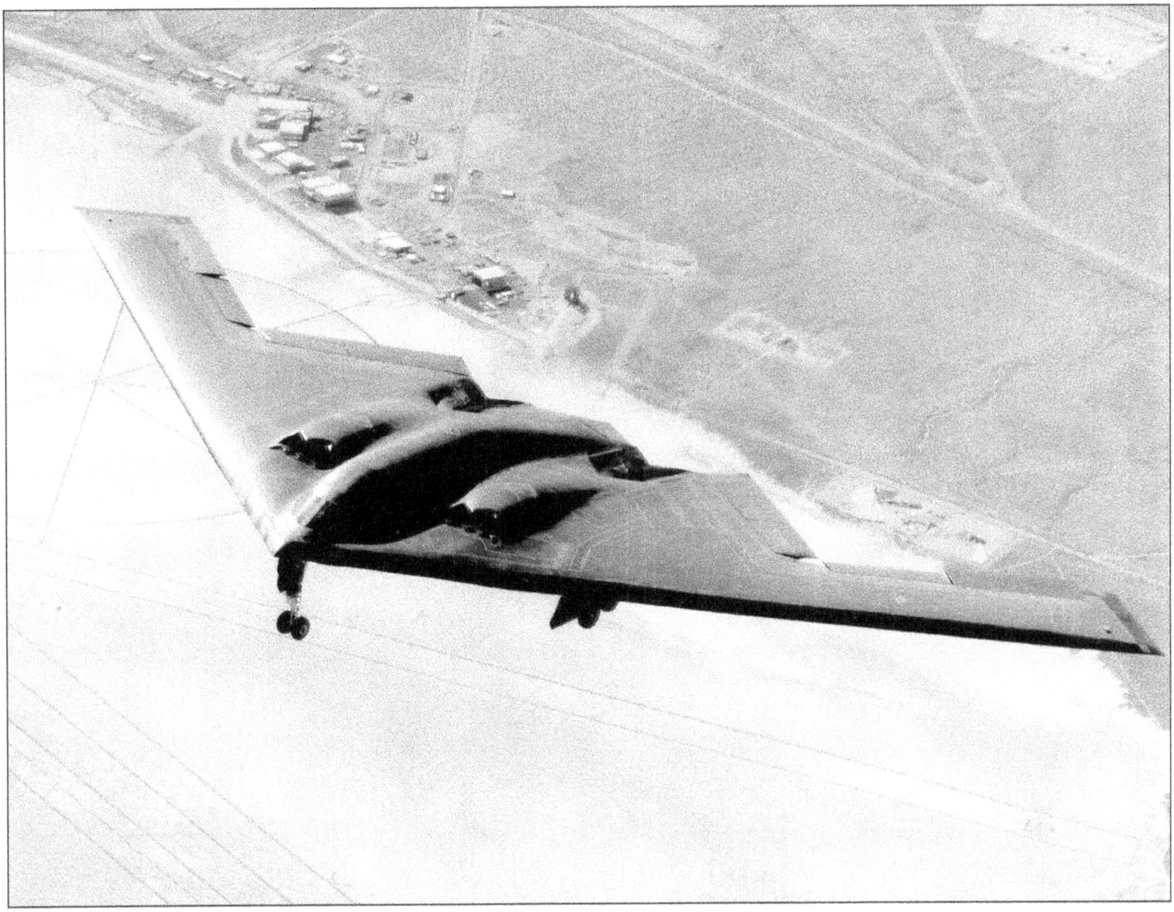

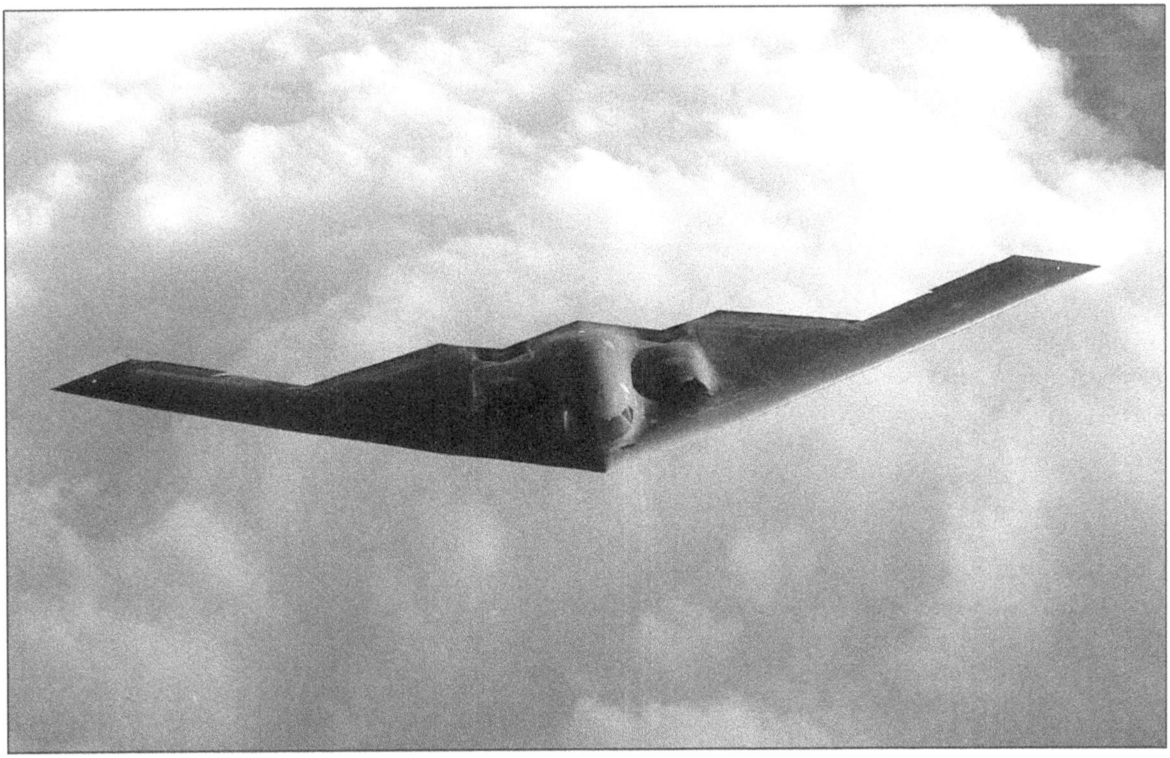

Previous page top: A B-2A passes over the dry lakebed runways at Edwards AFB, California, during a development flight. USAF **Previous page bottom: For such a large aircraft, the B-2A's tailless flying wing design makes the aircraft a hard target to detect visually, particularly from the frontal aspect.** Boeing **This page above: When viewed in close proximity to other large aircraft such as the USAF Boeing KC-10A Extender tanker/transport aircraft, the large size of the B-2A becomes evident.** USAF

The B-2A is not, however, completely invisible to detection sensors; it does have a radar, infrared and acoustic signature. The sensors can also emit a signature, which could betray the aircrafts position. However, the vast reduction in these signatures compared with non-stealth platforms makes it more difficult for air defence systems to detect, acquire, track or engage the B-2A. The protection afforded by the stealth capabilities enable the aircraft to fly at higher altitudes at much reduced risk even in a modern air defence environment which was absent in the Balkans.

Powered by 4 x General Electric F118-GE-100 non-afterburning fuel-efficient turbofan engines, each rated at 17,300-lb. thrust, the B-2A's un-refuelled combat radius is increased as it cruises at the more fuel-efficient higher altitudes. The USAF credits the B-2A with an un-refuelled range of 9600-km (6,000-nm).

The large wing of the B-2A casts a huge shadow as the aircraft crosses the threshold while landing at the end of a training flight. USAF

33

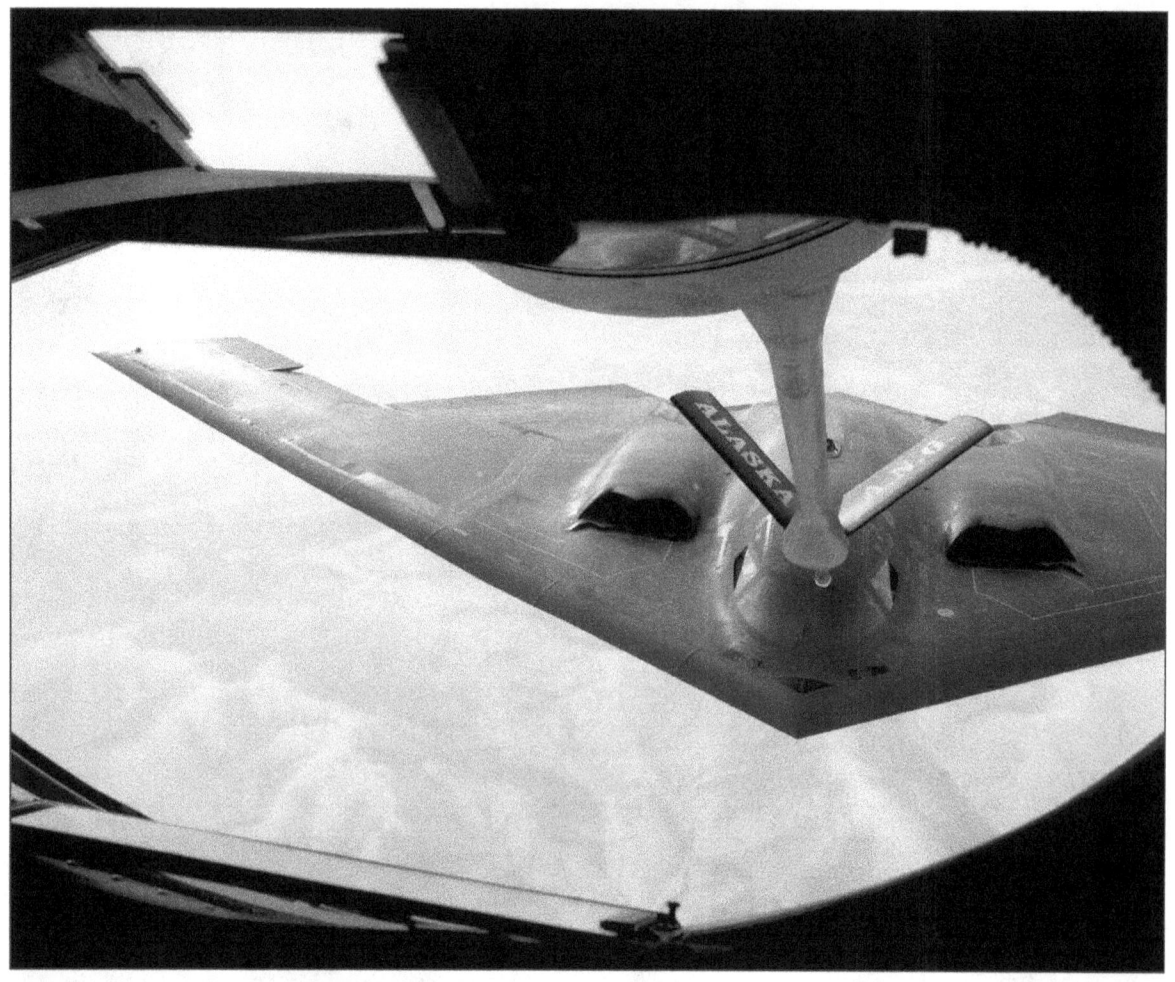

Previous page top: B-2A Spirit of Indiana is rolled out on 22 May 1999. At this time, the B-2A was involved in its first bombing campaign. Previous page bottom: B-2A Spirit of Alaska undergoes maintenance at its MOB (Main Operating Base), Whiteman AFB, Missouri.

Above: An Alaska ANG KC-135E refuels a B-2A over the snow-covered mountains of Alaska USAF

Whereas the B-52H had a crew of five and the B-1B has a crew of four, the B-2A has a crew of only two, the pilot occupying the left-hand seat and the mission commander occupying the right hand seat. The mission commander is also a pilot allowing alternate crew to rest during long-duration flights.

The B-2A is equipped with an advanced highly capable low-probability of intercept radar system, the Raytheon AN/APQ-181, which is integrated with a number of other advanced avionics and sensors to aid the bombers targeting and increase the aircraft's offensive and defensive capabilities.

Ordnance is carried in two side-by-side weapon bays, which can carry a combined total of 44,000-lb. of ordnance between them. The baseline conventional bomb load is sixteen 2,000-lb. GBU-31 JDAM's, which are carried and released from a rotary launcher in each bay.

While the conventional bombing role caught the headlines the B-2A's primary task remained as a nuclear bomber, whereby it can be armed with B61 and B83 gravity nuclear bombs under the SIOP (Single Integrated Operational Plan) mission. Other conventional weapons cleared for the B-2A include the M117 750-lb., MK 82 500-lb. and MK 84 2,000-lb. free fall gravity bombs, CBU-87/89/97 cluster bombs, MK 82 500-lb. sea mines and the AGM-154 JSOW (Joint Stand-Off Weapon).

A B-2A takes on fuel from a 351 ARS tanker in 1997. USAF

By the time of its operational debut the B-2A was a proven highly accurate bombing platform. The aircraft is equipped with a GATS (GPS-Aided Targeting System), which bestows the capability to cue guided weapons like the GBU-31 JDAM using the aircrafts APQ-181 radar. The GATS system can be used to refine target co-ordinates received from external sources such as the Northrop Grumman E-8C J-STARS (Joint-STARS) battlefield surveillance system, which can improve weapon impact accuracy compared to the bomb on co-ordinates mode. The GATS combined with GPS guided weapons greatly enhances the all-weather bombing capability of the B-2A.

The B-2A was designed for low-level penetration of heavily defended air space. By 1999, the Terrain Following/Terrain Avoidance system had been cleared for operation down to 600-ft altitude. However, low-altitude flight is seldom practised as the conventional bombing mission is conducted from medium and high altitudes. The main operational scenario for low-altitude missions would be when flying a SIOP mission, which would suffer from some limitations of the B-2A's Terrain Following/Terrain Avoidance system. Ongoing system improvements and new software releases were aimed at enabling the B-2A to meet the 200-ft. altitude flight capability using the Terrain Following/Terrain Avoidance system.

The tailless design of the B-2A contributes to the reduction in RCS (Radar Cross Section) of the aircraft and reduces weight. The design of the B-2A exhaust assists in shielding the heat signature from infrared detections systems. USAF

Top: The B-2A's were named after US States with the exception of the first aircraft, which was named Spirit of America. The Spirit of New York is seen during a training flight. Above: The Ghost like face of the cockpit area of Spirit of Alaska, serving with the 39th Bomb Squadron, 509th BW, is evident as the aircraft taxis with airbrakes open following a training flight on 22 November 2003. USAF

A B-2A with its undercarriage extended during a training flight in 1997. USAF

As the B-2A entered the 21st Century, the aircraft still fell short of the customer requirement in many areas including mission rate, LO (Low Observable) maintenance, 'deploy-ability' as well as limitations in the speed of the Mission Planning System, with the latter reducing the B-2A's capability to sustain combat operations when deployed.

While the B-2A performed well in Operation Allied Force, this was against a less than modern air defence system and by 2000; it was acknowledged that the principal threat to the aircraft's survivability was unsatisfactory DMS (Defensive Management System) performance. Improvements have been introduced increasing the capability of the DMS.

The first B-2A was publicly unveiled on 22 November 1988 when the aircraft was rolled-out from the production hanger at Northrop's Plant 42, Palmdale, California. The aircraft conducted its first flight on 17 July 1989, joining the B-2 Combined Test Force at the AFFTC (Air Force Flight Test Centre) at Edwards AFB, California, which was responsible for flight-testing the EMD (Engineering Manufacturing Development) aircraft. The flight test program continued until June 1997.

Initial plans to produce 130 B-2A's were shelved and the USAF eventually would receive only 21 of these hugely expensive aircraft. The unit, which dropped the Atomic bombs at the end of World War II, the 509th BW, was chosen as the sole operational B-2A Wing based at Whiteman AFB, Missouri, and the wings first B-2A was officially delivered on 17 December 1993.

By the end of 1999, sixteen B-2A's had been delivered to the latest Block 30 configuration, with earlier aircraft having been brought to this standard from earlier Block 20 standard. The last of the 21 B-2A's was delivered to the USAF in 2000.

B-2A Spirit
Engines: Four General Electric F118-GE-100 turbofan engines, each rated at 17,300-lb. thrust
Length: 20.9-m (69-ft.)
Wingspan: 52.12-m (172-ft.)
Height: 5.1-m (17-ft.)
Weights: 152634-kg (336,500-lb.) typical take-off
Speed: High subsonic
Range: Intercontinental un-refuelled
Ceiling: 15240-m (50,000-ft.)
Crew: Two
Payload: In excess of 18144-kg (40,000-lb.) of mixed ordnance

The AGM-86C CALCM (Conventional Air Launched Cruise Missile) has been used operationally in a number of conflicts since entering the inventory in 1991. An AGM-86C is loaded onto a B-52H at RAF Fairford during Operation Allied Force in March 1999. USAF

Boeing AGM-86C CALCM

From the early 1980's, the Boeing AGM-86B ALCM (Air Launched Cruise Missile) became the standard stand-off nuclear weapon for the B-52, allowing the large vulnerable bomber to retain a degree of survivability in the face of a dense Soviet Air Defence System. From 1991, the AGM-86C became the primary conventional stand-off weapon for the B-52G and later B-52H, being the longest-range conventional strike weapon in the USAF inventory.

The AGM-86 is a small winged cruise missile which is powered by a single Williams Research Corporation F107-WR-10 turbofan engine, which can propel the missile at sustained high-subsonic speed. When carried on the aircraft, the wings are folded to allow easier stowage. Once launched, the wings, folded tail surfaces and engine inlet, deploy for cruise flight.

The AGM-86B is capable of flying 'complicated' routes through the use of a terrain contour matching guidance system. For increased accuracy, the AGM-86C employs an on-board GPS system coupled to the INS (Inertial Navigation System).

The AGM-86B was developed to give USAF bombers a stand-off capability, removing the need to fly over defended territory on nuclear strike missions. This B-52H is shown with AGM-86 missiles in front of the aircraft and AGM-129 ACM (Advanced Cruise Missiles) on the wing stations. USAF

The B-52H can carry a total of twenty AGM-86B/C missiles – eight in the internal weapons bay mounted on a rotary launcher and six under each wing. When launched in large numbers, an AGM-86C cruise missile attack is difficult to counter with an enemy expending considerable effort and expense to even partially defend against such an attack scenario. The small size of the missile makes it hard for air defence radar systems to acquire let alone engage and unguided AAA systems have very little time to optically acquire and engage the missile when flying at ultra-low level.

In February 1974, the USAF issued contracts for the development and flight-testing of the AGM-86A, which was used for flight-test development, but did not enter full-rate production. In January 1977 the USAF began full scale development of the larger AGM-86B ALCM. Production of the initial batch of 225 missiles began in FY 1980, and the weapon was declared operational in December 1982 with the B-52G's of the 416th BW at Griffiss AFB, New York. A total of 1,715 AGM-86B missiles were eventually procured with the last weapon being delivered in October 1986.

Development of the AGM-86C CALCM began in June 1986, probably as a result of the US lacking a stand-off conventional strike capability that could be launched from CONUS based bombers, highlighted during the US skirmishes with Libya in the mid-1980's. Under initial CALCM contracts a small number of AGM-86B ALCM's were converted from their nuclear role to a conventional role. This saw the W-80 nuclear warhead removed and replaced by a 2,000-lb. blast fragmentation warhead. As the conventional role required greater accuracy than that required for the nuclear role, the AGM-86B's terrain contour-matching guidance system was replaced by an integrated GPS (Global Positioning System) coupled to the existing INS. The CALCM became operational in time to be used in the opening hours of Operation Desert Storm in January 1991.

During 1996/97, an additional 200 AGM-86B's were converted to AGM-86C CALCM configuration. These weapons were delivered to Block 1 standard featuring a new 3,000-lb. blast fragmentation warhead. Guidance was enhanced by the inclusion of a multi-channel GPS receiver and integration of a buffer box into the GPS receiver system. The existing Block 0 CALCM's were retrofitted with the improved avionics, bringing all in-service CALCM's to an identical standard electronically.

This still shows a Boeing AGM-86C CALCM milliseconds before impact with a target during a live fire test. Various impact angles can be selected including the almost vertical impact seen here. Boeing

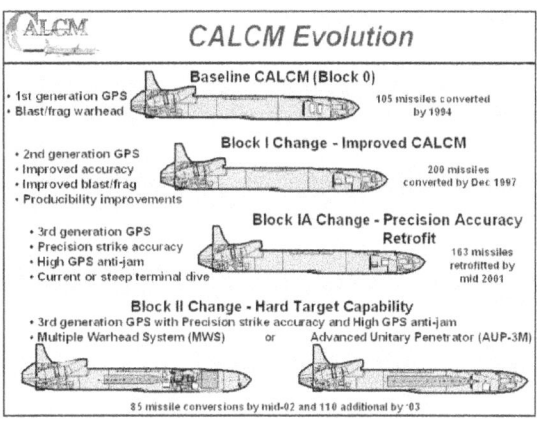

This chart shows the evolution of the CALCM from the baseline Block 0 to the Block II hard target capable missile. Boeing

While the development of the AGM-86C CALCM was kept secret, the AGM-142 Hap Nap was the public face of the program to give the B-52G/H a stand-off conventional strike capability. The Have Nap is a heavy missile that can only be carried on the B-52's external pylons. H Harkins

---

Boeing AGM-86C CALCM

Engine: Williams Research Corporation F107-WR-10 turbofan engine rated at 600-lb. thrust
Length: 6.3-m (20-ft. 9-in)
Weight: 1429-kg (3,150-lb.) Block 0
Diameter: 62.23-cm (24.5-in)
Wingspan: 3.65-m (12-ft.)
Speed: high subsonic
Range: 600-nm (nominal)
Guidance system: Litton INS element integrated multi-channel on-board GPS
Warhead: Block 0 (2,000-lb. blast fragmentation) Block 1 (3,000-lb. blast fragmentation)

In April 1998, a contract was awarded for development and production of the Block 1A CALCM, which utilises a precision accuracy kit incorporating a third generation GPS receiver and advanced navigation software and GPS anti-jam electronics module and antenna giving the missile a much higher degree of defence against GPS jamming. The first Block 1A missile conversion was delivered in January 2001, and the missile conducted its first flight in February that year. The two contracts for 322 CALCM's awarded to Boeing in 1999 included 132 missiles, which were to be delivered to Block 1A standard.

Lockheed Martin AGM-142 Have Nap

While the AGM-86C CALCM remained shrouded in secrecy, the USAF, in the 1980's, ordered the Israeli designed AGM-142 Have Nap as a conventional stand-off weapon for the B-52 to give the B-52 a long-range precision strike capability.

Have Nap is derived from the Israeli Popeye air to surface missile developed for the Israeli Air Force for use on tactical combat aircraft. The AGM-142 variant entered service with the USAF on the B-52 in 1989.

The AGM-142A is a development of the Israeli Rafael Popeye air to surface missile carried by tactical strike aircraft. Lockheed Martin teamed with Rafael to develop the Have Nap to arm the B-52. Lockheed Martin

Have Nap was designed for use against a wide-range of target sets including bridges, high-value military and industrial sites, bunkers and also against surface vessels.

The modular approach bestows multiple guidance modes and options to further increase accuracy and combat effectiveness. The AGM-142 had a claimed hit probability of 94% and the missile could be launched at stand-off ranges of around 50-nm then fly various flight trajectories, minimising exposure of the launch aircraft to potential ground defences. Launches can be conducted from low to high altitudes, with the higher altitude launches allowing greater range to be achieved. The missile benefits from mid-course autonomous guidance based on an inertial navigation system. The data-link antenna is located below the engine nozzle located at the rear of the missile. Once near the target, the missile then homes in on the aim point using an IIR (Imaging Infrared) or TV seeker head, which then guide the missile to the target. The IIR and TV seekers are interchangeable and can be selected and fitted to the missile prior to each mission. The target is destroyed using either blast fragmentation or hard penetration warheads, which are interchangeable.

AGM-142 Have Nap
Propulsion: Solid fuel rocket motor
Length: 190-in
Diameter: 21-in
Horizontal span, upper: 62-in, lower; 68-in
Vertical span: 42-in
Weight: 3,000-lb.
Warhead: 1,000-lb. class
Guidance: Inertial midcourse with IIR or TV in terminal phase

A B-52H drops a load of M117 750-lb. gravity iron bombs over a range. USAF

General Purpose Bombs

The M117 is an unguided 'dumb' general-purpose 750-lb. gravity bomb, which dates back to the Korean War and differs little from bombs employed during World War II. Normal fuses for the M117R are the mechanical M904 (located in the nose) or the M905 (in the tail).

Although developed primarily as a nuclear bomber, the B-2 can be used as a bomb truck. A B-2A drops a load of MK84 2,000-lb. bombs. Fifteen of the 16 internally carried bombs are visible. USAF

There are several different variants, including the basic M117 with a low drag tail designed for medium and high altitude release. The M117R (Retarded) uses a fin assembly, which can be optimised for either high or low drag release scenarios. During a low-altitude bomb-release the bombs tail assembly opens a quartet of large drag plates designed to rapidly slow the bombs descent allowing the launch aircraft to escape the blast zone. The M117D (Destructor) is configured similar to the M117R, but has a magnetic influence fuse, which allows the bomb to become a mine. This variant is released in a high-drag configuration and is used for shallow water mining or ground implant mining. Passing objects trigger the mines making the weapon completely indiscriminate.

The M117 was used extensively by the US during the wars in SEA during the 1960's and 1970's. The M117 was dropped in considerable numbers from USAF B-52G bombers during Operation Desert Storm in 1991, but the weapon was not employed during Operation Allied Force in 1999.

The MK 80 series of LDGP (Low Drag General Purpose) bombs developed in the 1950's have been used extensively in a number of conflicts. The MK80 series was designed to be more aerodynamic than previous generation general-purpose bombs like the M117. All of the MK80 family adopted a similar construction of cylindrical shape with conical fins, or retarders, designed for high-speed external carriage on bomber and tactical strike aircraft. The weapons are equipped with nose and tail fuses to enhance reliability and the bombs produce blast fragmentation and cratering effects. The casing of the MK 80 series is lightweight allowing some 45% of the bombs total weight to be explosive content.

No aircraft in history has carried as much ordnance internally on a single operational sortie as the B-1B Lancer, which can carry a total of 84 MK 82 500-lb. general-purpose bombs in the three internal weapons bays. No less than 72 bombs can be seen in this view of a Lancer dropping MK 82 bombs on a range facility. USAF

For low-altitude release the MK 80 series AIR bombs are fitted with a BSU-50/B high drag tail unit, whereby a 'ballute' air bag deploys, increasing drag and slowing the bomb rapidly, allowing aircraft conducting a high-speed low-altitude release to escape the bomb blast area.

The MK 82 is a 500-lb. bomb, the MK 83 is a 1,000-lb. bomb and the MK 84 is a 2,000-lb. bomb.

JDAM

JDAM (Joint Direct Attack Munitions) is basically a GPS-guided kit that can be fitted to existing 'dumb' iron bombs, turning them into near-precision guided munitions at a relatively low cost in defence spending terms. The baseline weapon is the GBU-31 which adds a JDAM GPS/INS guidance kit and a 1760A weapons interface to a MK 84 2,000-lb. bomb or a BLU-109 hard target warhead. The GBU-30 mates the same type of tail kit with the MK 83 1,000-lb. bomb.

During a conventional iron bomb attack the aircraft weapon system computer takes a number of factors into account such as wind velocity and altitude, and computes the weapon trajectory, positioning the aircraft at the best 'guessed' release point. With JDAM things are taken a stage further; target co-ordinates are programmed into the JDAM on the ground, although the co-ordinates can be changed in flight, allowing alternative targets to be attacked.

The crew can select impact angles between 10 and 30°. According to Boeing the flight path to the target can be programmed into the weapon allowing it to fly around the target and attack it from the side.

The need for a weapon in the JDAM class emerged after the 1991 Gulf War showed that targets obscured by smoke or cloud could not be designated for LGB (Laser Guided Bombs). During such conditions, even if a laser lock was achieved, it was often lost at some point during the bombs flight. The use of satellite guidance removed this problem, although this was achieved at the cost of reduced accuracy, which is why JDAM is often referred to as a near precision rather than a precision guided weapon.

JDAM is basically a tail and body kit, incorporating a GPS guidance system, that, when fitted to unguided weapons like the MK84 2,000-lb. bomb, converts them into 'near-precision' guided munitions. H Harkins

The first operational platform for the JDAM was the B-2A, which was declared operational with the 2,000lb. GBU-31 variant in 1998, and employed this weapon during Operation Allied Force from March 1999. USAF

In September 1995, McDonnell Douglas (now Boeing) was awarded a development contract for JDAM, with the weapon then scheduled for IOC in 1997. Flight-testing of bombs with JDAM kits commenced at Eglin AFB, Florida, in October 1996, with accuracy better than the 13-m (40-ft.) required by the specification being achieved. From March 1997, GBU-31 JDAM's were drop tested from a B-2A, followed by the other two heavy bombers, the B-52H and the B-1B. The weapon was also integrated onto USAF, USMC/USN tactical fighter aircraft, although limited bomb stocks saw the weapon remain the preserve of the B-2A during Operation Allied Force.

The development contract covered the purchase of some 650 kits and a LRIP (Low-Rate Initial Production) contract was awarded in 1998 covering a further 937 tail kits. The weapon entered operational service with the USAF in 1998, and was used operationally during operation Allied Force when B-2A's dropped hundreds of GBU-31's on targets in the former Yugoslavia.

A JDAM development weapon is seen just before impact with a retired Grumman A-6E target during development testing. NAWC-WD

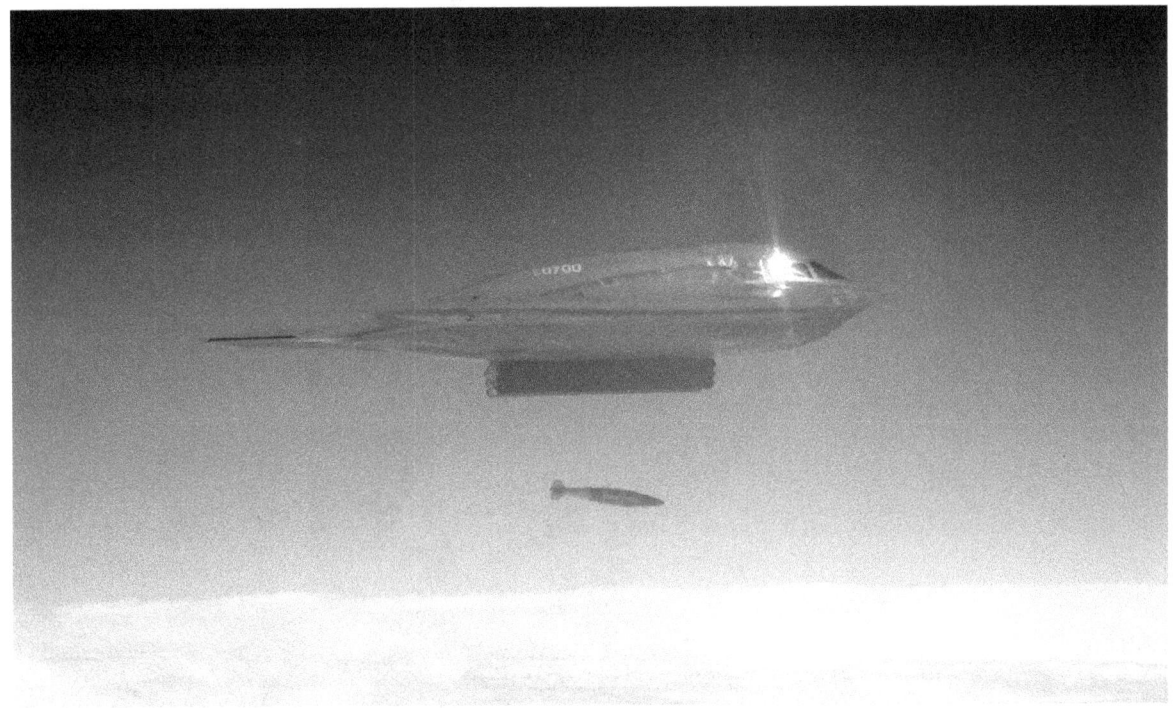

A B-2A drops a GBU-31 JDAM over a test range. USAF

Development of JDAM continues and kits have been produced for a number of weapons, including the smaller MK 82 500-lb. bomb. The US armed services had requirements for improved variants of the weapon with greater accuracy and these were further developed going into the 21st Century as the USAF/USN moved ever more towards reliance of GPS-guided munitions.

GBU-37

The GBU-37 is a GPS-guided 4,700-lb. class deep penetration bomb that was unique to the armoury of the B-2A. The weapon is guided to the target area along the same principles as the JDAM.

A GBU-37 was dropped by a B-2A for the first time on 29 May 1997. The weapon, which was fitted with a BLU-113-warhead, was released over the China Lake ranges near Edwards AFB, California. Following successful drop tests, the GBU-37 became operational with the B-2A that year as the only all-weather near precision "bunker buster" bomb in the US inventory. The B-2A can carry up to eight GBU-37's in its internal weapon bay. Four of these weapons were used against Serbian targets.

GBU-37
Guidance: GPS/INS
Power: Un-powered
Range: Depends on launch altitude, but typically around 5-nautical miles
CEP: 12-18 metres
Inventory: At least 128 units procured

JDAM became more or less the standard US 'smart' bomb. The benefits of JDAM include low acquisition costs and the ability to be used when weather conditions are not favourable for other systems. H Harkins

Chapter 2

Operation Allied Force

The USAF deployed B-52H bombers to RAF Fairford in October 1998 as part of NATO's planning for possible air attacks against the Federal Republic of Yugoslavia (Serbia). USAF

In early 1998, fighting between Serbian forces and the KLA (Kosovo Liberation Army) erupted across the Serbian Province of Kosovo as yet another phase in the long-running civil wars of the former Yugoslav republics, which began with the break-up of the country in 1991. Around a quarter of a million people were displaced and some 2000 Kosovo Albanians and around 1,000 Serbians, mostly civilians, were killed. In October 1998 a ceasefire was brokered, enabling displaced persons to return to their towns and villages, partly alleviating the potential of a catastrophic humanitarian crisis going into the harsh Balkans winter. An international monitoring mission was placed inside Kosovo under the auspices of the OSCE (Organisation for Security and Cooperation in Europe). While fighting receded, the ceasefire existed in name only, with both sides continuing to perpetrate acts of violence against the other.

In January 1999, violence flared up with 45 ethnic-Albanians killed on the 15th. In early 1999, a peace conference was held in Rambouillet, Paris, France, with both sides initially refusing to meet the terms laid out for a peaceful settlement. Although initially rejecting peace terms, the self-styled KLA (Kosovo Liberation Army) finally agreed as it became clear that NATO would launch air strikes against Serbia if the KLA accepted the Rambouillet accords and Serbia refused. The Paris summit ended with the suspension of peace talks on 19 March, with Serbia remaining defiant in the face of NATO threats to bomb. The OSCE withdrew from Kosovo as NATO finalised plans for the start of its bombing campaign.

A USAF B-52H lands at RAF Fairford in early March 1999. Below: A B-52H approaches to land at RAF Fairford in October 1998. USAF

The following day, Serbia launched a new phase of operation 'Horseshoe', moving ground forces into Kosovo, this apparently having two main objectives - attempt to defeat the KLA and to provide additional forces in the event that NATO launched a ground offensive from neighbouring Macedonia. The first objective also saw the Serbs step up attempts to force ethnic Albanians from their towns and villages.

NATO's campaign in the Balkans came at a time when the Alliance was desperately seeking a role to play on the world stage. Set up to defend the western powers against a possible attack from the Soviet Union, and later the Warsaw Pact alliance, with the end of the Cold War and the break-up of the Soviet Union, NATO was an alliance without an enemy to face. Facing criticism about its very existence, NATO was constantly expanding towards the Russian border yet appeared to lack any real role. Without a NATO alliance, the US could not justify basing large numbers of troops in Europe, together with massive quantities of equipment, including Armour and hundreds of combat and support aircraft. Indeed, even with the NATO alliance remaining in force, the justification for large US force levels in Europe was at the very least questionable to a public on both sides of the Atlantic. Desperately seeking a reason to exist, the Balkans campaign gave NATO a role to play at the very time the need for the alliance was under severe scrutiny. Survival of the alliance was probably more central to NATO's policy in the Balkans than any humanitarian mission to help the Kosovo Albanians, which, while suffering under Serbian rule, Kosovo was only one of a huge number of countries where the civil population was being repressed by their own or external governments. In many countries the death toll literally dwarfed that seen in Kosovo, yet NATO had no interest

A B-52H from the 20th BS, Barksdale AFB, Louisiana, at RAF Fairford on the eve of operation Allied Force. USAF

in a role in those countries in Africa where civilian deaths could be measured in tens of thousands and in the case of Rwanda in the mid-1990s, in excess of one million.

On the surface it appears that NATO was under the impression that a few days of bombing would cause the Serbian leadership to crumble and plead for peace talks. This school of thought may have had its roots in the experience of NATO air strikes on Bosnian Serb targets during Operation Deliberate Force in August and September 1995. While many accounts of the Bosnian war credit NATO air power as more or less single handed bringing the Bosnia Serbs to the negotiating table, the truth is rather more complicated. NATO air strikes were only a minor part of the military pressure being exerted against Bosnian Serb forces at that time. While still fighting with Bosnian Muslim forces, the Serbs had to contend with the artillery and other forces of the Anglo-French RRF (Rapid Reaction Force), which helped break the siege of Sarajevo. The artillery of the RRF was in action even on days when there were no NATO air strikes. At the same time, Bosnian Serb forces were reeling under the pressure of Operation 'Storm', a massive ground offensive launched by Croatian forces in the north west of the country.

NATO planned for a phased air campaign. Initial plans were authorised long before the Paris peace talks; as far back as October 1998. Phase 0 involved the gathering of assets for the assault. Phase 1 was designed to firmly establish air superiority over Serbia and Kosovo, creating a No Fly Zone south of 44° North latitude, and degrade command and control and the IADS (Integrated Air Defence System) over the whole of what was the Federal Republic of Yugoslavia. Phase 2 included attacks on targets in Kosovo and against Serbian forces south of 44° North latitude. Phase 3 would expand air operations over a wider range of 'high-value' military and security targets throughout the Federal Republic of Yugoslavia. Phase 4, which was not authorised by the North Atlantic Council, would have expanded the air campaign against a 'broad range' of targets north of the 44th parallel across the entire Yugoslav Republic.

Previous page: In the first days of the campaign, the B-52H detachment at RAF Fairford launched large numbers of Boeing AGM-86C CALCM's at targets in Serbia and Kosovo. Here, ground crew are in the process of loading an AGM-86 onto a B-52H in March 1999. Above: Following the long flight over water, a B-52H receives an anti-corrosion wash down after landing at RAF Fairford in March 1999. USAF

After the first month it became clear to the NATO leadership that the original approach to the execution of the campaign was not achieving the desired effect. Fundamental to this was the frequent inability to hit tactical targets in Kosovo. At the NATO summit in the United States on 24 April 1999, authorisation to widen the scope of the air campaign within the authorisation of Phase 2 was given to SACUER (Supreme Allied Commander in Europe).

Weather over Kosovo and Serbia was either completely unfavourable or marginal on the majority of days during the first two months of the campaign, causing many missions to be cancelled either before take-off or after aircraft had launched. As strike aircraft and support aircraft were operating from many different locations, strikes were sometimes cancelled because support aircraft could not launch. While aircraft could have flown below the cloud base, this was ruled out mainly due to the fact that Serbia's air defences against low-flying aircraft could have caused problems for strike aircraft, which would have been vulnerable to MANPADS (Man Portable Air Defence Systems) like the SA-7 and SA-18 as well as unguided AAA (Anti-Aircraft Artillery), and, at low altitudes, even small arms. Serbian forces shot down a number of UAV (Uninhabited Air Vehicles), which were flying at much lower altitudes than manned strike aircraft.

At the start of the operation NATO committed hundreds of combat and support aircraft at land bases in theatre and the CONUS, and on USN aircraft carriers in the Adriatic Sea. The bulk of the air assets were provided by the US, with USAF Lockheed Martin F-117 Nighthawk strike aircraft, Lockheed Martin F-16 and Boeing F-15E strike fighters, F-15C air superiority fighters and Fairchild A-10A Thunderbolt II ground attack aircraft. The initial USAF heavy bomber component comprised a force of B-2A and B-52H's.

The B-2A Spirit 'stealth' bomber was committed to operation Allied Force - the first time the bomber had participated in a combat operation. This B-2A is en-route to the target area on 27 March 1999. USAF

USN Northrop Grumman F-14 Tomcats strike fighters and USN/USMC Boeing F/A-18 Hornet strike fighters, along with a handful of USMC Boeing AB-8B Harrier II strike fighters were allocated to the operation. Backing up this large force of combat aircraft was a large force of support aircraft including air refuelling tankers, Boeing E-3 AWACS (Airborne Warning and Control Systems), Northrop Grumman E-8 JSTARS (Joint Strategic Targeting and Reconnaissance System) and a variety of electronic warfare, reconnaissance and defence suppression aircraft, including Northrop Grumman EA-6B Prowlers armed with Raytheon AGM-88 HARM (High Speed Anti-Radiation Missiles), which were employed throughout the campaign to prevent Serbian air defence radar systems from being able to effectively track and engage NATO aircraft. A host of other platforms employed HARM, including USAF F-16's, USN F/A-18's and German Air Force Tornado ECR (Electronic Combat and Reconnaissance aircraft.

HARM has earned a reputation for being ineffective and easily fooled by countermeasures while in the air. However, the weapons poor hard kill record in relation to the number of missiles launched is offset by the fact that when the enemy air defence system goes off line to force HARM to break lock, the missile has partially done its job by preventing the radar system from targeting friendly aircraft.

The only other anti-radar missile system used during the campaign was a handful of BAe Dynamics (now MBDA) ALARM (Air Launched Anti-Radiation Missile) launched from RAF Panavia Tornado GR.1 strike aircraft - ALARM apparently proving to be more effective than HARM. Tornado GR.1's were also used to strike targets with free fall and laser guided bombs along with RAF Harrier GR.7 strike fighters. Other NATO nations provided a variety of combat aircraft, including F-16's, F/A-18's, Alenia AMX, Tornado strike aircraft and Tornado F.3 air defence fighters, the latter supplied by Italy which operated the aircraft on lease from RAF stocks. So benign was the Serbian airborne threat that Britain did not provide any interceptors of its own, the available space at air bases being more appropriately allocated to other assets such as strike aircraft.

A Boeing B-52H trails its drag chute as it passes a line of Boeing AGM-86C CALCM (Conventional Armed Cruise Missiles after landing back at RAF Fairford, Gloucestershire, United Kingdom, following a mission in support of Operation Allied Force. USAF

When the operation commenced the USN had 8 Frigates, Destroyers and Cruisers armed with BGM-109 TLAM-C and TLAM-D cruise missiles. The TLAM-C is armed with a conventional unitary warhead, while the TLAM-D is armed with conventional sub-munitions. Only Block III TLAM's were expended during the campaign. Mission planning for cruise missile strikes was conducted in the US and then forwarded to the launch platforms in theatre. The Royal Navy also launched a handful of TLAM's from HMS *Splendid*, a Trafalgar class submarine.

As with Operation Desert Fox, strikes against targets in Iraq, a few months earlier, the US placed a huge reliance on cruise missiles while conducting the early part of its bombing campaign. The depletion of AGM-86C CALCM stocks during the campaign, and usage over Iraq in December 1998, left the USAF with only 70 operational CALCM's by the time the campaign ended in June 1999. To overcome this shortfall, funding was allocated to convert an additional 322 nuclear armed AGM-86B ALCM's to conventional armed AGM-86C CALCM standard. The huge numbers of Raytheon BGM-109 TLAM's used in operation Desert Fox and Allied Force saw $431 million allocated to convert an additional 624 nuclear armed TLAM's to conventional armed TLAM configuration.

The NATO onslaught began on 24 March 1999, under the code name Operation Allied Force, when hundreds of NATO combat and support aircraft, supported by ship and submarine launched BGM-109 TLAM and AGM-86C CALCM's launched from Boeing B-52H bombers, struck a number of pre-planned targets. The first targets were struck by CALMC and TLAMS just after 19.00 hours followed by strikes by tactical aircraft.

The B-2A, teamed with the GBU-31 JDAM GPS guided bomb, allowed NATO to accurately strike fixed targets above the cloud base during periods of adverse weather. USAF

Although the Serb air defence system was active, the various aircraft defensive systems, and the support afforded by defence suppression systems, considerably eased the threat to the bombers. A wealth of data on the Soviet era systems operated by Serbia had been accumulated in previous campaigns in the 1990's, particularly Operation Desert Storm, the 1991 Gulf War against Iraq, allowing a number of advanced countermeasures to be developed to combat the threat from obsolete SAM (Surface to Air Missile) systems of the SA-3 and SA-6 types and their derivatives operated by Serbia. These counter measures proved to be as invaluable over the Balkans as they had been over Iraq.

While many accounts give Serbian all-out attempts to shoot down NATO aircraft, throwing everything but the kitchen sink at them, the US DoD (Department of Defence) 'After Action Report' actually disputes this, claiming that Serbia had "husbanded" its anti-aircraft missiles to sustain its defence against the air assault. The DoD claim is supported by NATO documentation and reports released during the campaign.

In the lead-up to the commencement of operation Allied Force the USAF pre-positioned B-52H bombers and munitions at RAF Fairford. During the conflict additional B-52H's rotated in and out of Fairford as other aircraft returned to the US. USAF

The unmistakable sight of a B-52H – the huge vapour trails evident when flying at altitude. USAF

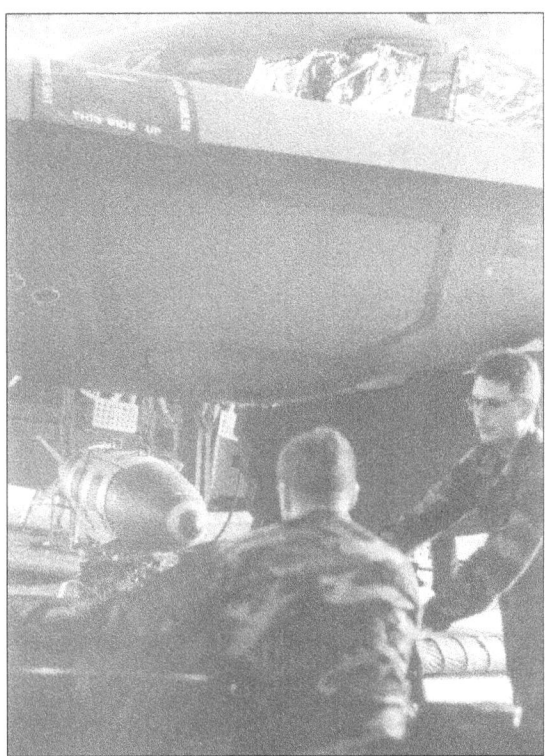

Ground crew load GBU-31 2,000-lb JDAM GPS guided bombs onto a B-2A at Whiteman in the early days of the conflict. USAF

A Boeing GBU-31 JDAM is transported to a B-2A during arming at Whiteman AFB, Missouri. The B-2A was the only platform armed with JDAM during the campaign. USAF

While many accounts state that Serbia fielded a modern sophisticated integrated air defence network, this premise would only be true if it were applied to a 1980's airborne threat. Even by the standards of countermeasures available in the early 1990's, let alone 1999, Serbia's Air Defence Network would have to be considered as woefully obsolete. However, even an obsolete system was capable of 'chance' success, as shown when an F-117A Nighthawk 'stealth' strike aircraft was shot down by a Serbian SAM near Belgrade a few days into the campaign, despite the fact that NATO aircrew were ordered to stay above 15,000 ft., which kept them out of the engagement envelope of much of the air defence system and degraded the performance of those systems that were capable of engaging aircraft at these altitudes.

NATO records state that most non-infrared guided Serbian SAM launchings were optically guided, or ballistic (unguided), making it highly unlikely that missiles unmolested by countermeasures would find targets. On some days no confirmed SAM firings were recorded, on others it was ones and two's. NATO stated Serbian "Air Defence Ineffective", not surprising since it was vintage 1960's and 1970's technology, with few updates beyond technology levels available in the 1980's

One day NATO reported "13 x U/I missiles and 1 x shoulder launched missiles" being launched, this being one of the busier days. On days SA-6 missiles were launched NATO reported only small numbers, 2 x being the norm, although on the 24 hours covering the period of the night of 2 May 1999, when a USAF F-16CG was shot down by a SAM, NATO reported that there were 6 x SA-6 missiles launched, although only one was guided, the rest being ballistic launches.

Later in the campaign there were short burst were NATO reported an "Increase in air defence activity" with "numerous SAM launches in last 24 hours." This would be followed the next day by a "Decrease in air defence activity".

For day 44 only 3 SAM launches were reported over the previous 24 hours. Day 45, 8 SAM launches in previous 24 hours. On day 46 and 48 only "Light Air Defence Activity" was reported; these being a few examples.

In late May, 33 SAM's were reported launched in one 24 hour period, followed the next day by only 4 SAM launchings, this being followed within a day or so by 18 SAM launchings in a 24 hour period, the latter recorded on 31 May. This report was followed by another report for the same day that only 2 SAM firings were noted.

In late March, ACC began preparing a small force of B-1B's for commitment to the campaign. This aircraft is seen being armed at RAF Fairford in early April 1999. USAF

Initially ACC committed four Block D and a single Block C B-1B to the operation. These aircraft were transferred to RAF Fairford on 1 April 1999. USAF

The NATO report for the 24 hours covering 2 June showed 4 SAM launchings and light AAA, and a the report for 24 hours covering 4 June showed 3 SAM launchings. By this time the writing was on the wall, Serbia's defences had proven ineffective while NATO's bombing campaign had met with mixed effectiveness. Fielded targets were proving very difficult to accurately target and NATO was running out of fixed strategic targets, many strikes simply being revisits to targets already struck.

The Serbian Air Force, even on paper was hopelessly outclassed, facing an enemy possessing overwhelming numerical and technical superiority. In the early days of the campaign a number of sorties were generated, particularly by MiG-29 'Fulcrum' fighters, a small number being shot down by NATO fighters, USAF F-15 Eagle and Dutch F-16 Fighting Falcons. Primary air to air armament for the majority of NATO fighters was the Raytheon AIM-120 AMRAAM (Advanced Medium Range Air to Air Missile) active radar guided air to air missile and AIM-9L/M Sidewinder infrared guided air to air missile.

While the B-2A was designed to be extremely difficult to detect by radar, the hugely expensive bombers went nowhere near hostile territory during Allied Force without the protection of dedicated defence suppression aircraft like the EA-6B Prowler (top). USAF

As with Operation Desert Fox – bombing of Iraq - three months before, the only weapon dropped by the B-1B was the MK82 500-lb. unguided bomb, thousands of which were dropped on area targets such as Serbian airfields. USAF

Above: This trio of B-1B's are being prepared for a bombing mission at RAF Fairford on 1 April 1999. Right: A B-2A breaks from the tanker during a mission in April 1999. USAF

While the campaign commenced with fewer than 500 combat aircraft committed, this eventually grew to over 1,000 as the campaign progressed and additional assets were deployed from NATO nations. The USAF deployed combat aircraft at a number of bases in theatre, and B-52H bombers were forward based at RAF Fairford in the UK. The USN/USMC deployed aircraft on aircraft carriers in the Adriatic Sea and at land bases.

While NATO put on a unified face there were certainly cracks below the surface, particularly with regards to which targets could legitimately be attacked. Not all NATO nations provided airborne assets for the campaign; however, eventually over 300 non-US NATO aircraft were committed to the operation.

As well as the forward deployment of B-52H bombers, the USAF committed the Northrop B-2A Spirit 'stealth' bomber to combat operations for the first time. Although the stealth qualities of the B-2A were not mission critical considering the obsolete nature of the Serbian IADS (Integrated Air Defence System), the 'Spirit' was one of only a few aircraft integrated with the Boeing GBU-31 JDAM (Joint Direct Attack Munitions), which was a GPS guided bomb which can be used at night or in adverse weather conditions from above the cloud base. The limited stocks of JDAM, which had only just entered production, meant that the B-2A was the only platform that was allocated this weapon, allowing NATO to continue to hit targets when adverse weather prevented the use of other weapons such as laser-guided bombs

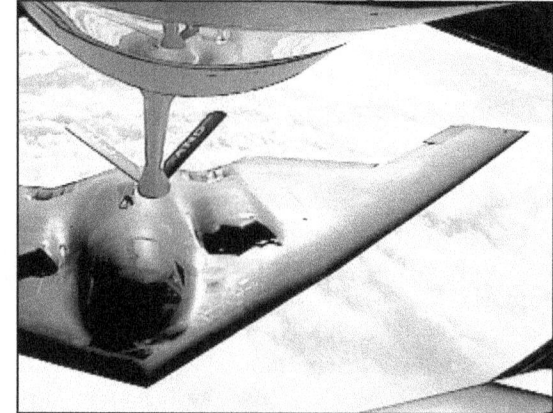

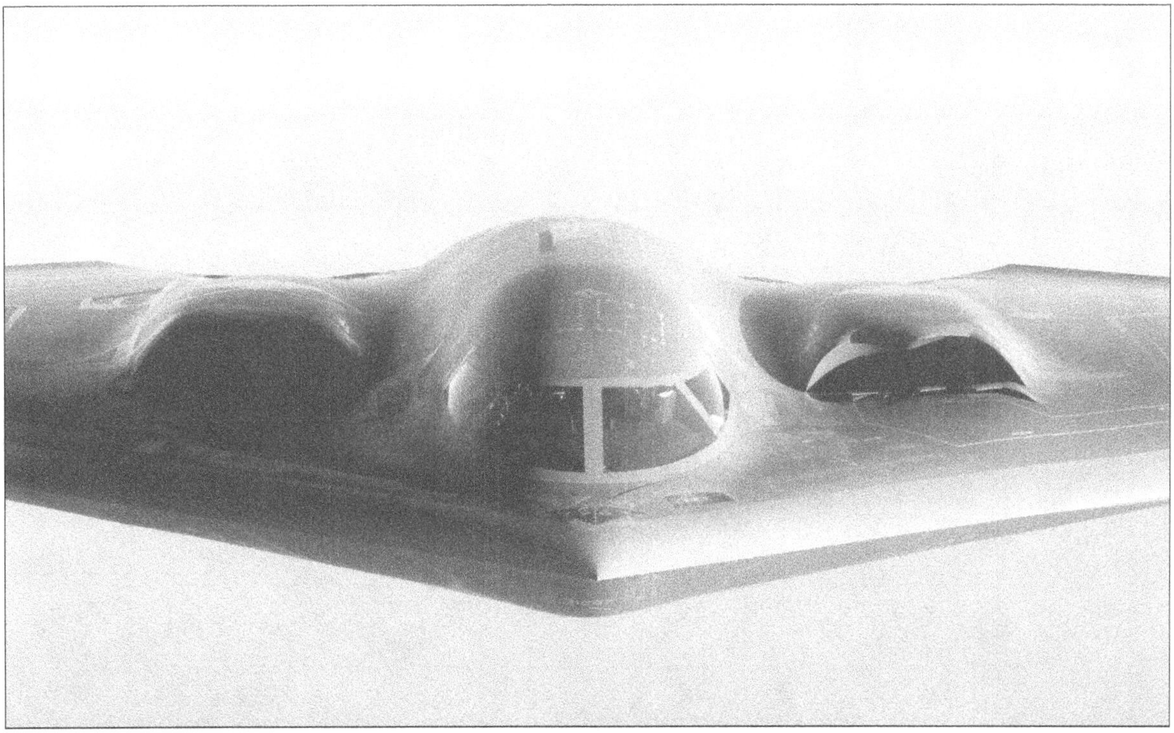

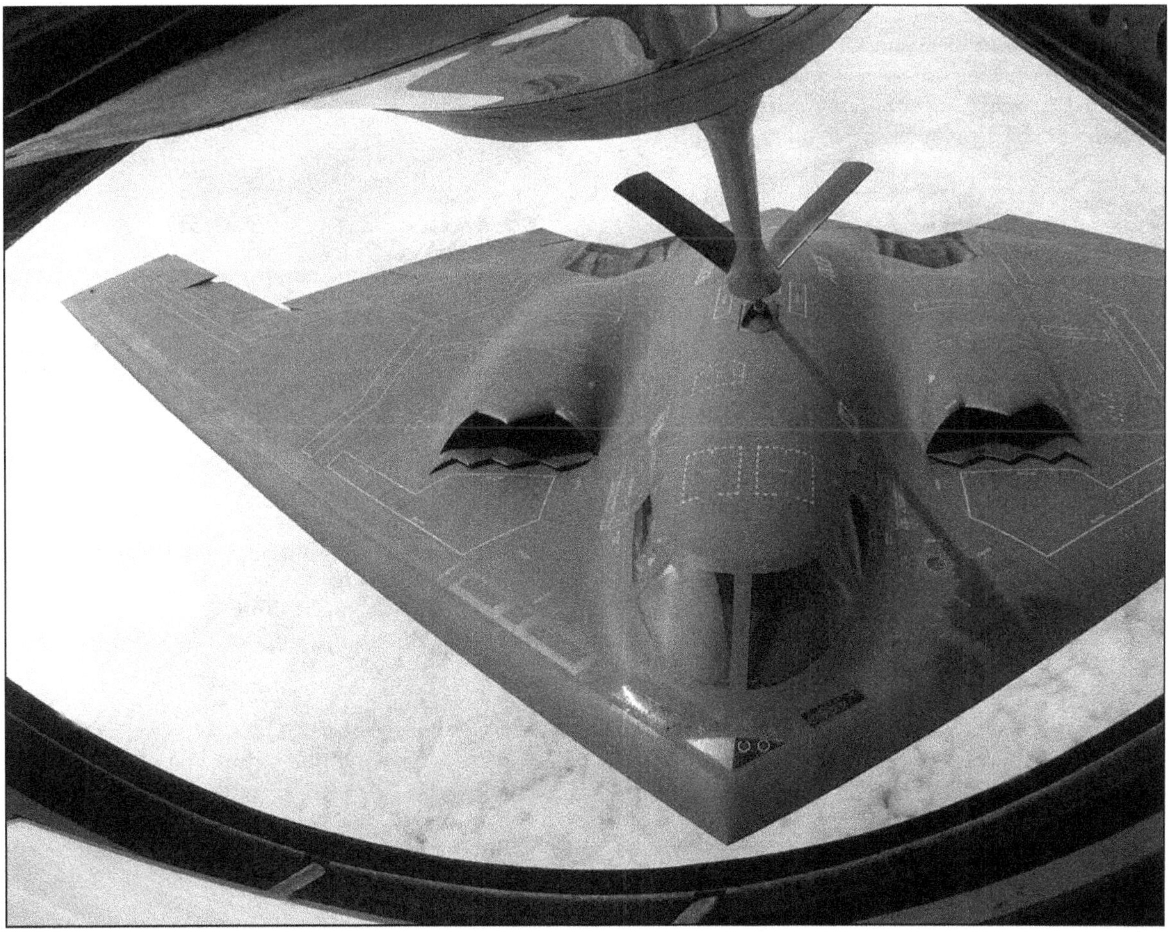

Previous page: A head-on view of a B-2A (top) during a bombing mission on 27 March 1999. This B-2A 'Spirit' (bottom) is seen hooking-up to a tanker during a mission on 6 April 1999. USAF

This page above: At the time operation Allied Force was launched, the Boeing GBU-31 JDAM had not long since entered production. The limited stocks meant that only the B-2A employed the GPS-guided all-weather bombs over the Balkans. Here ground-crew technicians are in the process of loading JDAM's onto a B-2A at Whiteman AFB. USAF

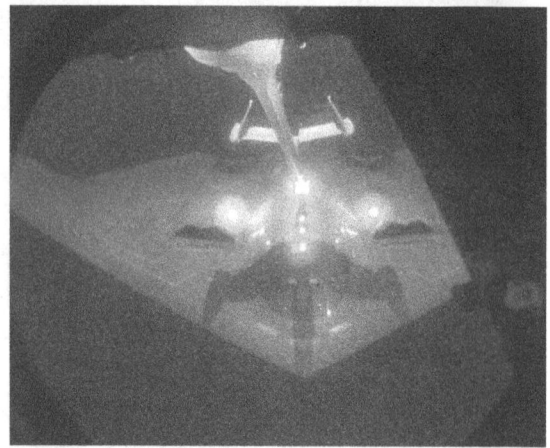

During the Allied Force campaign the long-haul missions conducted by the B-2A from Whiteman AFB required considerable tanker support. A B-2A conducts a night-time air to air refuelling during a bombing mission on 10 May 1999. USAF

Left: Planning for B-2A missions over Serbia and Kosovo began months before the campaign was launched. Targets were pinpointed and programmed, allowing practise missions, including air to air refuelling, to be conducted in the simulator at Whiteman. USAF

Top: A B-2A conducts an engine warm-up prior to a bombing mission on 23 April 1999. Above: B-2A missions were normally launched in pairs, with both aircraft crossing the Atlantic Ocean on the outbound leg to Europe together. This offered both crew mutual navigational support during the mission. USAF

GPS-Aided Targeting

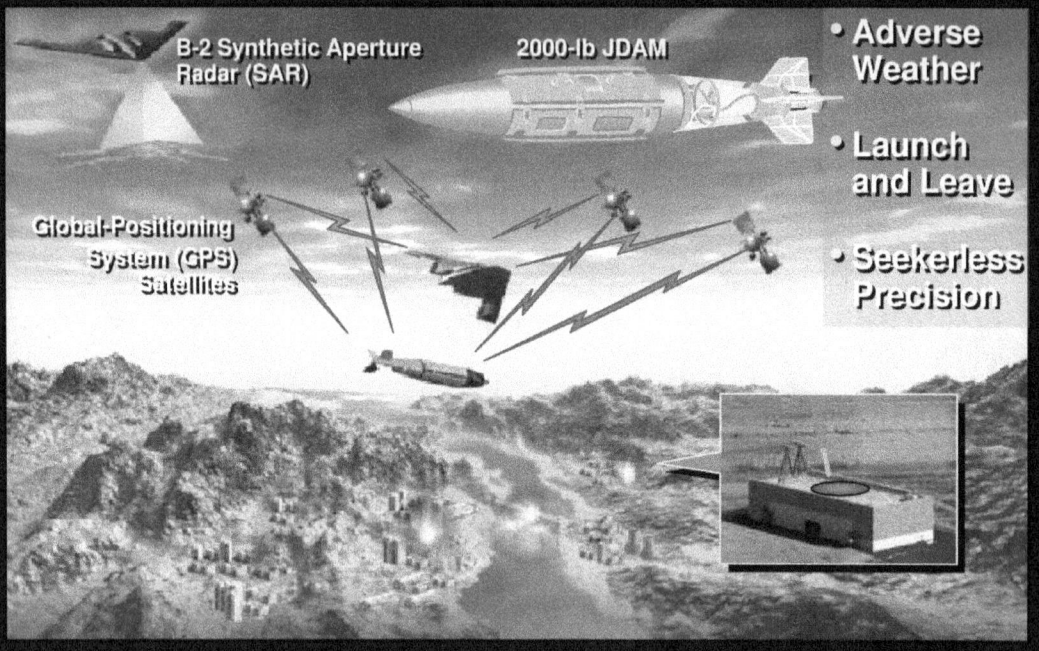

- Adverse Weather
- Launch and Leave
- Seekerless Precision

GPS-Aided Targeting System (GATS)

- ○ Automated Functions
- ■ Crew Functions

1. Select GPS Constellation
2. Enable GATS Mode & Command Imaging
3. Designate Aim Points
4. Updates Weapon(s)
5. Compute Second Update Parameters
6. Execute Second Update
7. Select Automatic Delivery Mode — Weapons Release
8. Weapons Use GPS

2 Radar Looks Eliminate Target-Location Error

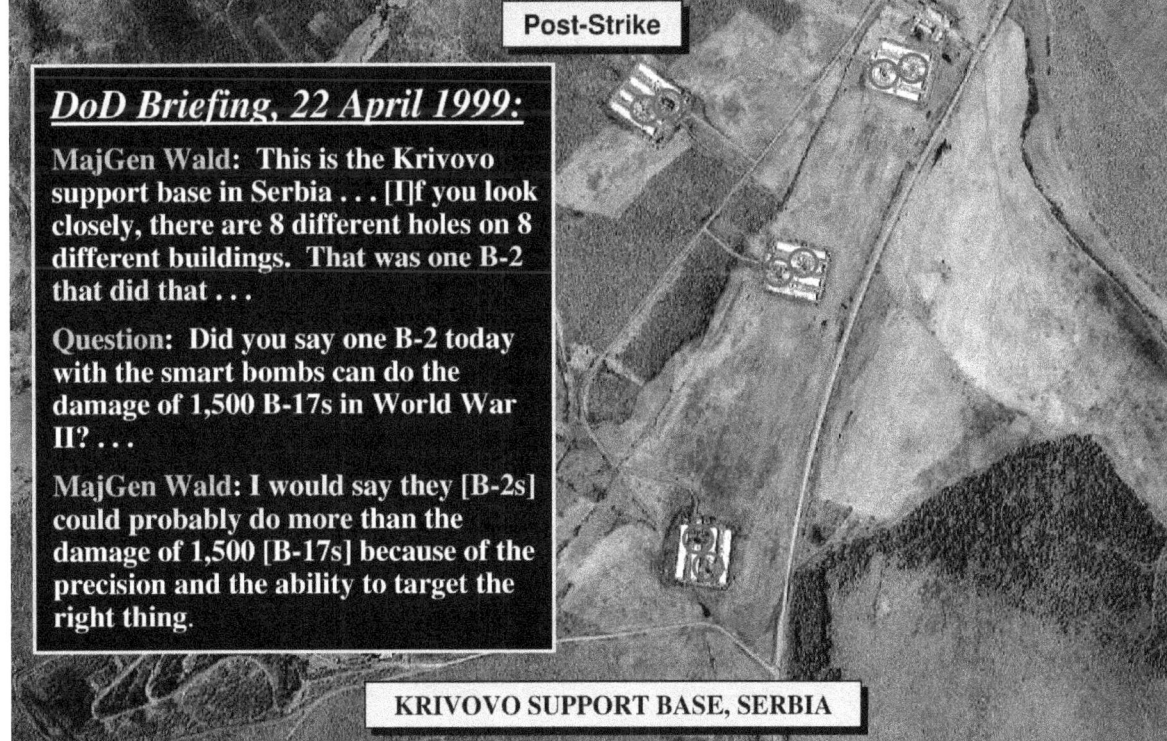

Multiple Aim-Points per Pass

NORTHROP GRUMMAN Analysis Center

Post-Strike

DoD Briefing, 22 April 1999:

MajGen Wald: This is the Krivovo support base in Serbia . . . [I]f you look closely, there are 8 different holes on 8 different buildings. That was one B-2 that did that . . .

Question: Did you say one B-2 today with the smart bombs can do the damage of 1,500 B-17s in World War II? . . .

MajGen Wald: I would say they [B-2s] could probably do more than the damage of 1,500 [B-17s] because of the precision and the ability to target the right thing.

KRIVOVO SUPPORT BASE, SERBIA

17 July 1999

Previous page top: **A B-2A takes on fuel over the Atlantic Ocean en route to the target area over Serbia.** USAF Previous page bottom: **Taken from a briefing from July 1999, this slide shows a post-strike image of the Krivovo Support Base in Serbia following an attack by a B-2A in April that year. The image shows 8 buildings, each of which was struck by a single GBU-31 JDAM released by the single B-2A.** Northrop Grumman

This page: **The B-2A performed well during the campaign, hitting targets in weather conditions that prevented other manned platforms from operating effectively.** USAF

Figures vary from one period to another, but it is considered that the 509th BW had an average of nine B-2A's operationally available during the campaign. Other B-2A's were available for normal tasking such as training. At the outset of operations the USAF assigned eight of these for operations over the Balkans with at least six being available at any one time. Aircraft not assigned to operational missions were used to continue training programs and conduct testing. The sufficient availability of pilots and aircraft allowed the 509th to have all the assets to be "perfectly prepared" for each mission. However, it has been acknowledged that had the requirement been to generate sorties in excess of those conducted, then the unit would have found sustaining the operation to be much more difficult.

There was no requirement for forward basing the B-2A fleet during the campaign. However, this would have been necessary if a higher tempo of operations was to be attained. Had this been implemented then a procedure known as 'employ on the deploy', would have been used, in which a B-2A would fly from Whiteman to the target area, release its weapons then recover at a forward base where it would be turned around and rearmed before flying to another target, release its weapons before returning to Whiteman AFB in the US. This type of operation would have allowed the B-2A fleet to generate additional sorties, but allow the vast support infrastructure to largely remain at its home base.

Months before Operation Allied Force began, the B-2A was prepared for use against targets in the Balkans. Many fixed location targets in the Balkans had been catalogued and programmed into weapon system trainers and simulators. This allowed strikes on planned targets to be rehearsed long before they were actually flown.

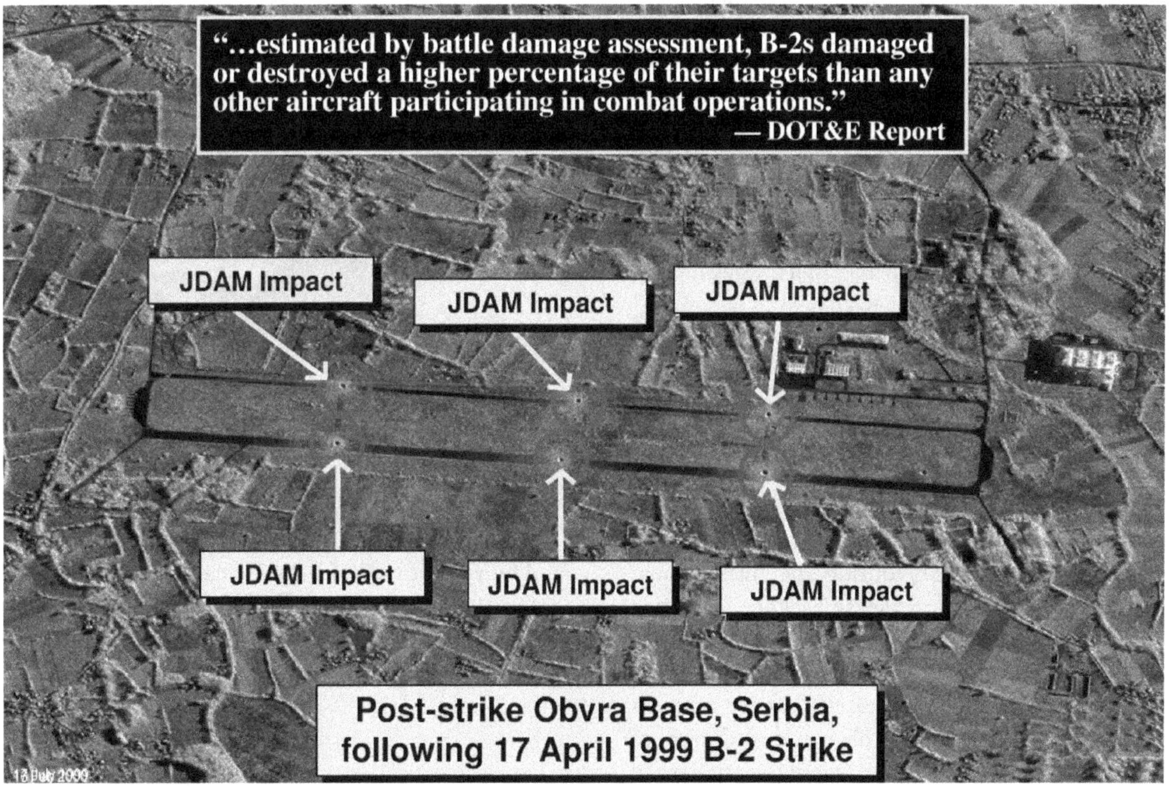

The Bomb Damage Assessment photographs above are testament to the accuracy achieved by the B-2A/JDAM combination during the campaign. USAF/Northrop Grumman

The Allied Force campaign proved a success for the B-2A force which flew 49 sorties, dropping 656 GBU-31 2,000-lb. JDAM's and four GBU-37 4,700-lb. class 'bunker buster' GPS guided bombs for a combined total of 660 weapons. The aircraft attacked a variety of fixed location targets. USAF

It has been suggested that a B-2A mission compares to a space launch mission in comparison to the psychological preparation, simulations and the incessant verification of checklists. While this may be a gross over exaggeration, the B-2A mission planning is a lengthy procedure, being conducted over several days. Around four days ahead of a mission, the crew receives GPS coordinates and imagery of a target, which are then checked against synthetic aperture radar imagery during the mission just prior to weapon release. The advance information of each mission allowed the pilots to build-up a flight plan, which included air to air refuelling, route through air defence systems to the target area, the bomb run and departure from the target area. The evening prior to a mission a B-2A crew would act as a backup launch spare for the mission. On the day a mission was to be flown, pre-flight inspection and final planning was conducted. The pilots were not involved in this procedure.

The vapour trail of a B-52H can be seen from the cockpit of another B-52H en-route to their weapons release point during an Allied Force mission. USAF

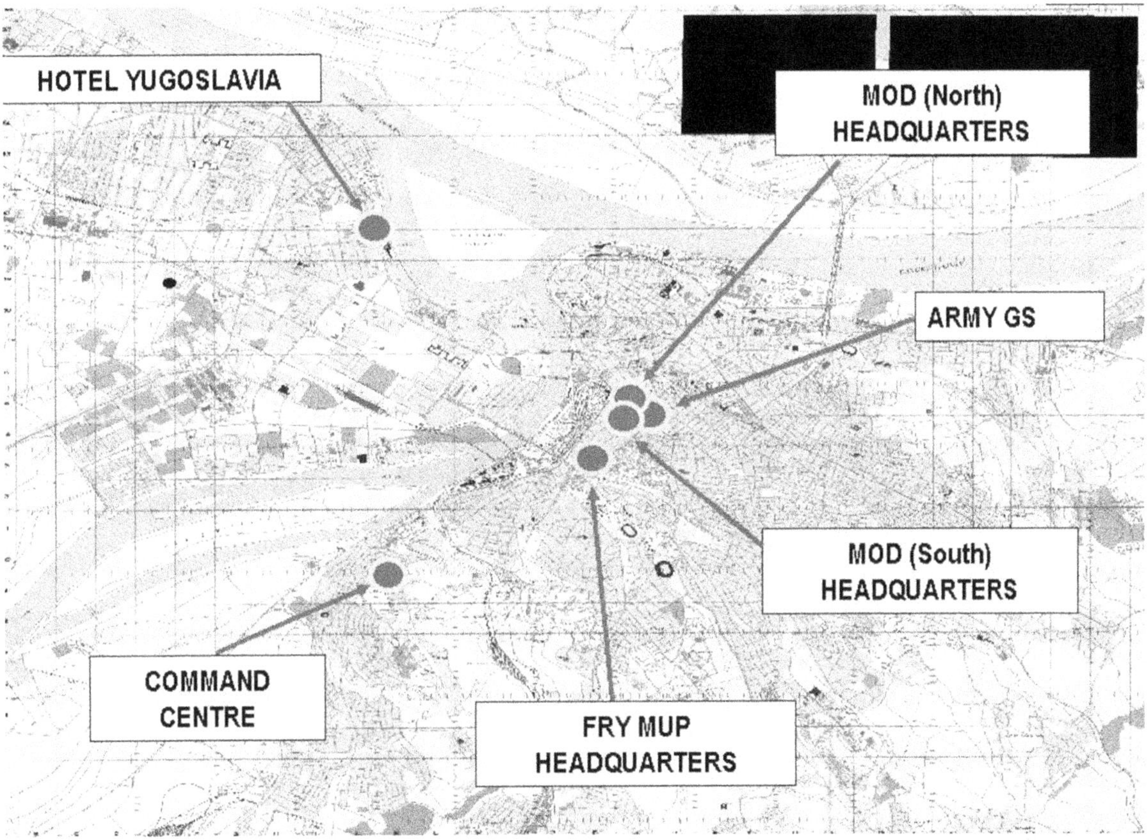

Map 1:
- HOTEL YUGOSLAVIA
- MOD (North) HEADQUARTERS
- ARMY GS
- MOD (South) HEADQUARTERS
- COMMAND CENTRE
- FRY MUP HEADQUARTERS

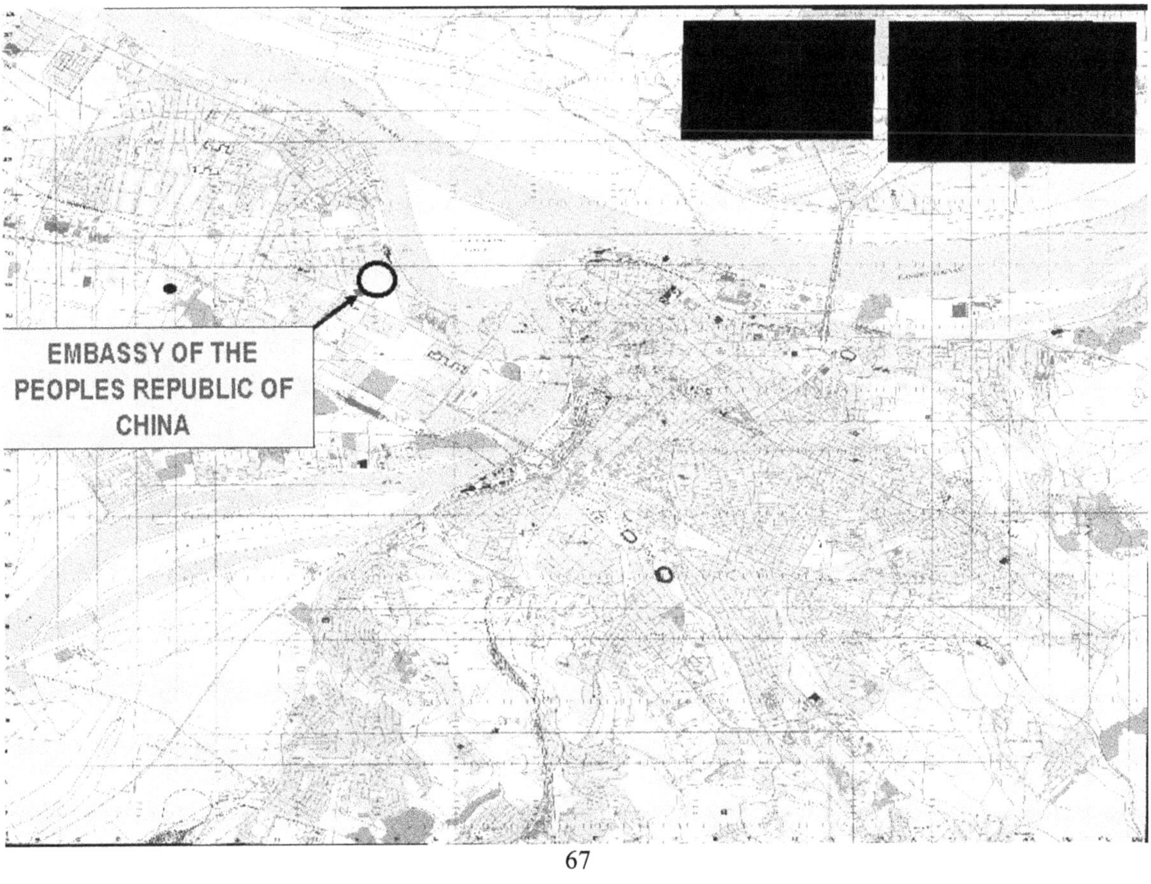

Map 2:
- EMBASSY OF THE PEOPLES REPUBLIC OF CHINA

Previous page: Maps showing various military targets in Belgrade along with the Hotel Yugoslavia (top) and the position of the Chinese Embassy (bottom). NATO **This page above: A B-52H about to touch down at the end of a bombing mission against Serbian targets. Right: A Boeing B-52H crosses the threshold at RAF Fairford during a bombing mission in May 1999.** USAF

B-2A missions were normally launched in pairs, the aircraft taking-off and crossing the Atlantic together, even if they were assigned to strike separate targets in different parts of the country. The aircraft would refuel in flight over the Atlantic and again just prior to entering the operation zone. During the long transit to and from the target zone, B-2A crew slept in shifts with beach loungers being used to allow the crew to relax. These loungers fitted perfectly into the space located just behind the mission commander's station. Other comforts afforded the crew during the flight included the ability to change clothes, eat warm food and wash using wet towelling.

During the approach to the target area the B-2A's synthetic aperture radar generated a picture that was almost photographic in quality and detail. This image was then checked against pre-mission intelligence imagery for identification of the target. The GPS coordinates were then verified via the GATS (GPS-Aided Targeting System), which allowed the B-2A commander to choose aim points on a specific target even if it was obscured by cloud. If necessary, target coordinates were updated before being fed to the JDAM via an aircraft to weapon umbilical cord. During bomb release the bomb bay doors would open once for each individual bomb release, then the weapon would steer to the target area.

Top and above: With CALCM stocks running low the B-52H force moved to conventional bombing armed with MK 80 series unguided iron bombs. Aircraft are seen taxiing at Fairford armed with MK 80 series bombs on the under wing stores stations. USAF

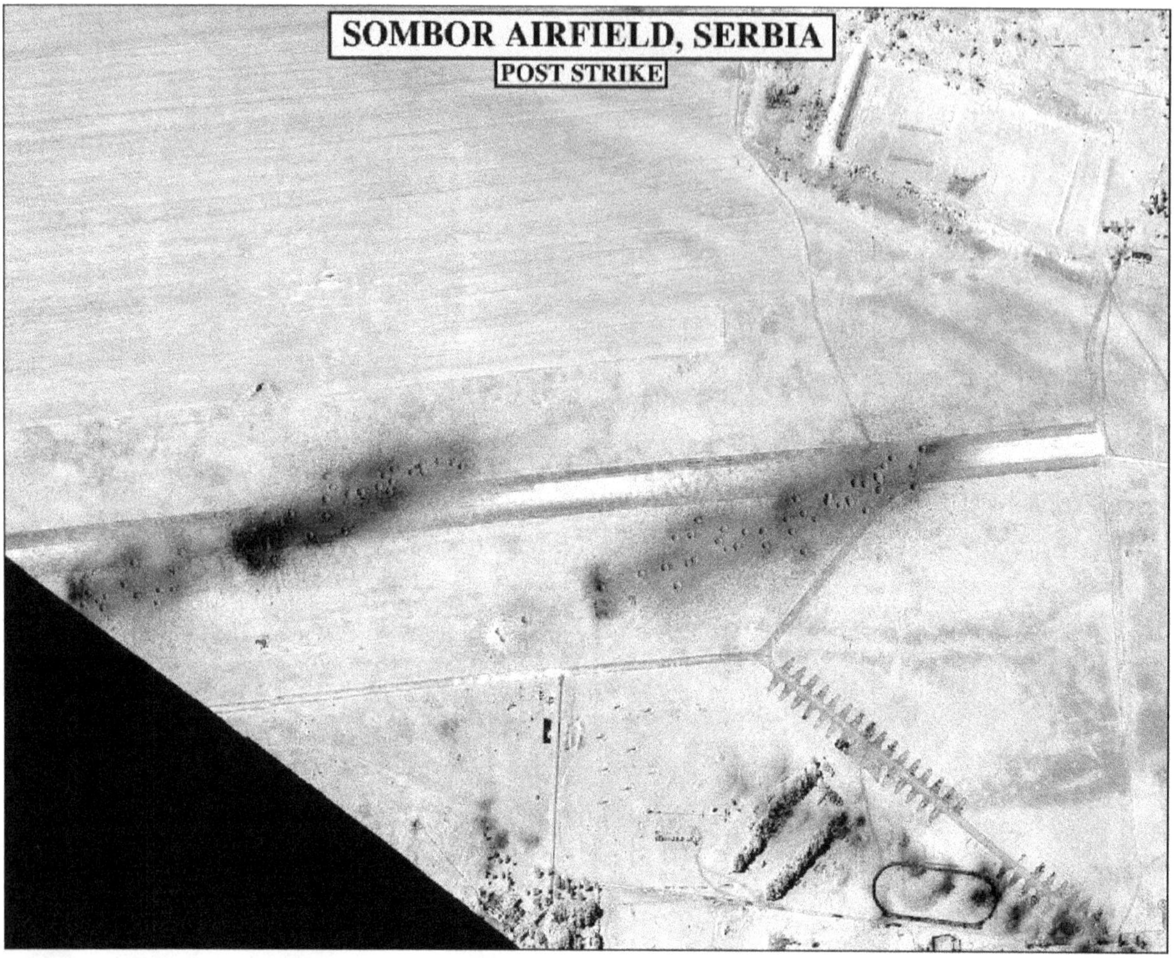

SOMBOR AIRFIELD, SERBIA
POST STRIKE

Above: Much of the B-52H/B-1B effort was directed against fixed area targets such as airfields. This BDA imagery shows extensive damage to the runway at Sombor airfield in Serbia after a visit from USAF bombers. A strike on the aircraft dispersal area at bottom right of image was less successful, almost completely missing the parking area. Right: The main runway and taxiway at Obrva airfield in Serbia, cut following a bomber strike. NATO

With JDAM the B-2A could attack 16 targets in 16 different locations during the same sortie, this being practised on at least one and possibly more occasions. B-2A pilots claim they were never detected over hostile airspace, although this probably meant that they were never targeted by radar, which is somewhat different to being detected. Serb radar emitting to detect other non-stealthy systems may well have picked up the B-2A's, although this appears not to have been in time to allow a successful SAM engagement.

Following weapons release, the B-2A's departed the combat zone and headed for home with the aid of two more in-flight refuelling's before landing back at Whiteman AFB after over 30 hours in the air.

The crater scared surface of Sjenica air base in Serbia resembles a lunar landscape following a number of air strikes by strategic bombers. As the campaign progressed NATO strike aircraft hit the same targets over and over again as there was a lack of suitable targets and Serbia would not yield. NATO

During the campaign, the 509th BW worked on plans to step up the tempo of B-2A operations, however, these did not materialise as SACEUR choose not to exercise any requirement for additional B-2A missions.

The B-2A carried 16 x 2,000-lb. GBU-31 JDAM's on rotary launchers in the internal weapons bay. The fuse for each JDAM was selected before the mission was launched allowing a variety of time delays ranging from before impact, impact or after impact. B-2A operations over Serbia were conducted exclusively under the cover of darkness. The aircraft flew in two-ship formations and alone. The B-2A's did not operate in synergy with other strike platforms; however, the aircraft did conduct strikes as part of a larger force often dropping the opening bombs of such attacks. The aircraft were required to stick to pre-arranged times for both their arrival and departure from the designated target areas. During the heavy bomber campaign against Serbian airfields, the B-2A was used to accurately crater portions of runway and taxiways before the B-1B and B-52H bombers arrived to drop huge loads of unguided ordnance on the airfield. The aim was to restrict the movement of Serbian aircraft in an attempt to trap them in the open, making an easier target for the B-1B's and B-52H's. During one such sortie, a B-2A was used to crater two separate runways at two separate airfields.

NIS BASE, SERBIA
POST STRIKE

Above and below: Two BDA photographs of Nis airfield in Serbia showing extensive damage to the runway. As can be clearly seen, many of the strikes missed any significant area of the base, however, the sheer volume of ordnance being deposited on the base resulted in a number of hits on the runway and taxiways. NATO

BOMB DAMAGE MORINA AREA, KOSOVO
POST STRIKE

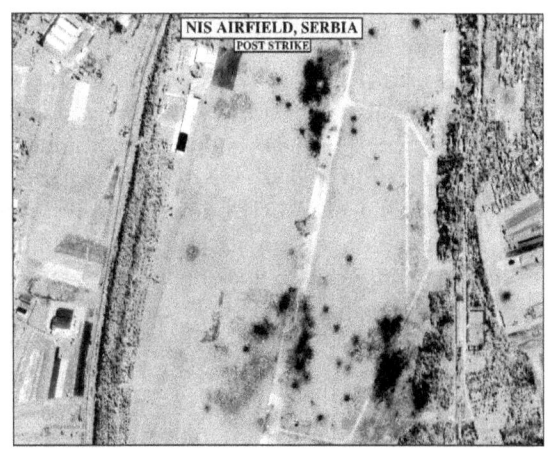

NIS AIRFIELD, SERBIA
POST STRIKE

Above: This area of countryside shows considerable scarring following a USAF heavy bomber strike. NATO

This B-52H is seen during a bombing mission over the Balkans on 26 May 1999. USAF

While not being directly interwoven into strike packages with other tactical combat aircraft, the B-2A's did not operate alone. The aircraft were supported by defensive platforms such as F-15C Eagle fighters sweeping for enemy interceptors and airborne jammers including Northrop Grumman EA-6B Prowler electronic warfare, defence suppression aircraft, which could provide jamming and lethal SOAD (Suppression Of enemy Air Defence) capability by launching Raytheon AGM-88 HARM missiles at emitting radar systems.

The use of JDAM, combined with the B-2A advanced mission systems, made the aircraft the most accurate all-weather inhabited platform available to the Allied Force commanders. JDAM was released from distances of around 15 miles from the target, removing the need for the B-2A to expose itself to some defences. The bombs received updates from the INS using updates from the GPS, which guided the bombs to the target area via movable tail fins. Once released, the JDAM is totally autonomous allowing the B-2A to turn away from the defended area.

The success of the B-2A/JDAM combination during Operation Allied Force saw the USAF seek funding to increase production of JDAM from 500-per month to 700-per month, allowing for around 10,500 JDAMs, to be included in the inventory by fiscal year 2002. The lack of facilities and capability for forward basing saw funding provided for pre-positioning aircraft spares, JDAM kits and the purchase of special aircraft shelters to facilitate forward basing requirements. Other capability improvements planned after Allied Force was to provide the crews with the capability to conduct mission planning en-route to the target in real-time.

During the course of the conflict, 51 pilots flew the B-2A on operations. Most flew only a single mission with a few pilots flying two missions and one pilot flying three missions. With crew fatigue deemed not a serious consideration due to the low mission rate, focus was on the mission capable rate of the aircraft itself. When low-observable maintenance was excluded, mission capable rate for the B-2A was around 75%, although this dropped to around 60% when low-observable maintenance was taken into consideration. USAF records state that every single B-2A mission began on time and only one aircraft had to abort its mission due to an in-flight mechanical failure. Once the aircraft had returned to base the problem was rectified and the aircraft was mission ready within 15 minutes. Another two missions were cancelled after take-off because some NATO partner nations withheld permission to attack the targets.

Ground crew secure AGM-86C CALCM's in the internal weapons bay rotary launcher of a B-52H at Fairford on 2 May 1999. Although the B-52H embarked upon a conventional unguided bombing campaign later in the conflict, the CALCM was still used in smaller numbers. USAF

While the B-2A was hailed a success during the campaign, it was not without its problems. The ART (Actuator Remote Terminal), which drives the B-2A's FBW (Fly-By-Wire) control surfaces, suffered a high failure rate because of an airflow problem affecting the mission capability of the fleet.

The B-2A Wing encountered a lack of 'supply assets' for the aircraft's ART. To solve the problem a team of engineers from the System Engineering Branch of the B-2 Program Management Division at Oklahoma Air Logistics Centre, Tinker AFB, Oklahoma, was dispatched to Whiteman AFB to train personnel for ART repair, allowing the B-2A fleet to continue flying during the campaign.

By 8 April 1999, the B-2A fleet had flown more than 12 missions and over 500 JDAM's had been delivered by 5 May, sometimes in adverse weather. On the night of 8 May 1999, a B-2A Spirit dropped three GBU-31 JDAM's on the Chinese Embassy in Belgrade. This incident would prove to be the most controversial of the entire campaign. In the days after the attack NATO gave a number of conflicting accounts as to why the building had been bombed. NATO eventually settled on a 'mistake' as the excuse for the incident, claiming it had mistaken the Embassy building for the Directorate of Supply and Procurement building. The day after the attack a US official told the media that the CIA (Central Intelligence Agency) had supplied inaccurate information regarding the target. However, a NATO spokesman when pressed claimed that NATO had known where Embassy buildings were located in Belgrade, stating quite clearly "Yes, of course we know where the Embassies are."

The official line settled upon that the CIA gave faulty information may have been correct, however, what remained hard to accept for many was the official line that this was simply a mistake. The Chinese Embassy had been in the location for four years and could even be found on tourist maps of the city, which could be picked up by anyone. This, combined with the fact that, as mentioned above, a NATO spokesman confirmed that NATO knew where the Embassies were, threw further doubt on the 'mistaken identity' excuse.

Four B-52's (top) taxi at the start of a mission over the Balkans. There were around eleven B-52H's in residence at Fairford at any one time during the campaign. However, the number of aircraft committed to the campaign was greater, as aircraft rotated to and from the US. USAF

The extensive CIA assets combined with the extensive military intelligence gathering assets at the US and NATO's disposal made it seem incredulous that no one in the entire exhaustive target selection process spotted a simple mistake about where the Embassy was. All targets were supposed to have been approved by all NATO nations of the North Atlantic Council, all of which would have had intelligence to confirm or repute whether a target was legitimate or not.

Top: A B-52H sits on the apron at RAF Fairford in May 1999 as a B-1B Lancer lifts-off on a bombing mission. Above: For much of the later part of the campaign, the B-52H called on its huge load carrying ability to deliver thousands of unguided bombs. A row of bombs on pallets awaits loading as a B-52H taxis past. USAF

Of the three USAF strategic bomber types employed during the campaign, the B-52H was the most versatile in terms of weapon load. The large Stratofortress was the only one of the three to employ standoff missiles and joined the B-1B in delivering huge quantities of unguided bombs. USAF

There has been reports that at least some of the US B-2A missions flown direct from the US were not approved by NATO, and speculation that the 8 May mission may have been one such mission. What is known is that several missions did not receive authorisation to release weapons, as some NATO members would not give their approval.

This BDA image of Ponikve airfield in Serbia shows a line of bomb craters, from 500 lb. weapons dropped by USAF bombers, cutting across the main runway. To the right of the crater line is a larger crater possibly caused by a GBU-31 JDAM dropped by a B-2A. NATO

What brought additional suspicion on the incident being a deliberate attack on Chinese sovereignty was the fact that this mission was claimed to have been the only one in which the CIA was directly involved in the target selection. The Directorate of Military Procurement is hardly the kind of target, which would require CIA involvement, at least no more so that a military barracks or a vehicle depot.

During the course of the 79-day campaign, the B-2A fleet flew 49 sorties, equating to only 1% of combat sorties, but they delivered 11% of ordnance to targets. The B-2A dropped 656 GBU-31 2,000-lb. JDAM's with a claimed 98% effectiveness. The weapons delivered resulted in a claimed 87% of the assigned targets being either destroyed or damaged. The USAF claims that 90% of the JDAM's dropped by the B-2A during the conflict landed within the prescribed 40-ft. from the target. B-2A's also dropped four GBU-37 4,700 lb. bunker buster bombs during the conflict. These weapons penetrate deep into the target before exploding.

There were a total of 53 ATO (Air Tasking Orders), 34 of which contained B-2A's. One mission was scrubbed because of technical problems. Targets for the B-2A included elements of Serbia's air defence system, command and control facilities, airfield runways and aircraft taxiways, communications, road and rail bridges, and other infrastructure target sets.

The USAF claims that the B-2A destroyed 33% of Serbian targets during the first eight weeks of operation Allied Force.

Although the first variants were introduced to service almost half a century before, in 1999 the B-52H remained the USAF's premier strategic bomber. USAF

During the campaign, the USAF claimed that the B-2A force maintained its primary role as a nuclear bomber under the SIOP (Single Integrated Operation Plan).

Often criticised because of its labour intensive maintenance for the radar absorbing coatings, the USAF claimed the B-2A required only minor additional effort for the low observable materials. The average turnaround for the B-2A was around one day, with the longest turnaround taking four days and the shortest four hours. The long turnaround time was necessitated because of the time required for curing within the LO (low-observable) print and tape requiring time to dry and harden after being applied.

Mission capable rate during Operation Allied Force was 43% compared with the requirement for 60%. MMH/FH (Mean Man Hours/Flight Hour) during the campaign were 14.03 compared with 24.57 during FOT&E (Follow On Test & Evaluation) through December 1998. Sortie generation rate was 0.15 from MOB (Main Operating Base) against a requirement for 0.55 from a deployed location. There were no released figures for the requirement from the MOB,

Acknowledging that the B-2A is not invisible to radar, but low observable, the need for a Link-16 secure digital data link was acknowledged as it would allow the B-2A to share data with other tactical and strategic aircraft in-theatre.

This B-52H from the 96th BS, 2nd BW, is seen at Fairford on 25 May 1999 as the bombing campaign was in its third month. USAF

One important finding of B-2A operations during the campaign was that aircraft deployability still did not meet operational requirements. Among the major obstacles to forward deployment was the need for aircraft shelters to allow LO (Low Observable) maintenance to be conducted, as well as a requirement for an extensive support equipment acquisition infrastructure. This requirement prompted the acquisition of deployable shelters allowing future forward deployments as it was realised that the need for forward deployment was urgently required if the B-2A was going to be capable of meeting required response times and sortie generation rates.

B-52H

The B-52H was the first real visible sign of US ACC strategic bomber force preparations for bombing missions against targets in the Balkans. Seven B-52H's from the 2nd BW, Barksdale AFB, Louisiana, were deployed to RAF Fairford in October 1998. As the diplomatic war of words between the western powers and Serbia continued, the bombers were returned to the US within a few weeks of their arrival at Fairford. By late February 1999, seven B-52H's were again resident at Fairford as perpetrations for NATO's planned air campaign against Serbia began in earnest.

The first B-52H mission of Operation Allied Force began when eight of the giant bombers lifted off from RAF Fairford on the morning of 24 March 1999. Each aircraft carried eight AGM-86C CALCM Block 1 missiles in their internal weapons bays. Another mission was launched two days later. Following weapon release, four of the aircraft involved in this mission then continued flying direct to the Continental US, while the remainder returned to RAF Fairford.

The B-52H's operating from Fairford changed regularly as aircraft would return to the US and be replaced at Fairford by different B-52H's. This allowed the B-52H's rotating back and forwards to the UK to transport additional CALCM's on the bombers from the US to Fairford. Three B-52H's also departed from Diego Garcia in the Indian Ocean, ultimately bound for Fairford, carrying CALCM's. These aircraft had initially been retained at Diego following the Anglo-US four-day bombing campaign against Iraq in December 1998.

Top: The variable-geometry B-1B brought a supersonic bomber capability as well as the largest bomb carrying capability of the USAF bomber trio. This B-1B is seen getting airborne on 28 April for a bombing mission. Above: A B-1B from the 77th BS, 2nd AEW, gets airborne at the start of a bombing mission from Fairford on 26 April 1999. USAF

At the time of operation Allied Force the USAF B-1B fleet was undergoing a block cycle upgrade, and the type was initially sidestepped as NATO miscalculated Serbian doggedness. When the B-1B was committed from late March, five aircraft were sent to Fairford to operate alongside the B-52H in the conventional bombing role armed with 500-lb. MK 82 unguided bombs. USAF

A 77th BS B-1B departs Fairford on 3 May 1999. The B-1B brought enormous bomb carrying capability to NATO's air offensive, albeit unguided. USAF

From the high tempo of CALCM launches in the first few days of the campaign, these weapons were used progressively less as stocks ran low. The sparing use of CALCM's was reserved for targets that could not be struck by conventional ordnance during bad weather. As cruise missile stocks were husbanded, the B-52H's resorted to dropping 'dumb' iron bombs as well as turning to another stand-off missile in its inventory, the Lockheed Martin AGM-142 Have Nap. While eight AGM-86 cruise missiles can be carried on a rotary launcher in the B-52H's internal weapons bay, the B-52H cannot carry the AGM-142 internally. These weapons were carried externally on the HSAB wing stations, either two on each pylon or one missile and an AN/ASW-55 datalink pod for the aircraft to missile data link interface. Only two AGM-142's were launched during the campaign, apparently achieving poor results.

During conventional bombing raids the B-52H was normally configured to carry a total of 45 x MK 82 500-lb. bombs in the internal bomb bay and on the wing stores stations. The B-52H's also apparently dropped small numbers of the MK 84 2,000-lb. free fall iron bombs. A total of 18 of these weapons could be carried, however, it is likely that smaller numbers of these weapons were carried along with a larger number of MK 82's. While the B-52H was equipped with GPS, the use of free fall unguided weapons was far from ideal for anything other than area bombing.

B-1B

While the B-2A Spirit brought an all-weather day or night near-precision strike capability and the B-52H provided a long-range stand-off precision strike capability, neither type could compete with the B-1B for sheer numbers of bombs carried. The B-1B Lancer was initially sidestepped for operation Allied Force as the fleet was undergoing a modernisation program. However, when it became clear that Serbia was going to be a tougher nut to crack than NATO planners had initially expected, the USAF supplemented the B-52H force flying out of RAF Fairford with the enormous load carrying capability of the B-1B.

A B-1B is seen being prepared for a mission shortly after its arrival at Fairford on 1 April 1999. USAF

Of the 93 B-1B's in the inventory in March 1999, only six had been modified to Block D standard under the CWUP (Conventional Weapons Upgrade Program). The Block D upgrade allowed aircraft to deliver Boeing GBU-31 2,000-lb. JDAM GPS-guided bombs and Lockheed Martin WCMD (Wind-Corrected Munitions Dispenser) cluster bombs. However, these weapons were new to the inventory and while the B-2A was armed predominantly with JDAM, the B-1B was left reliant on unguided MK 82 500-lb. iron bombs. Even if sufficient JDAM kits had been available the B-1B would probably not have employed this weapon as the MPS (Mission Planning System) was classed as unsatisfactory as it did not account for wind. The B-1B's also lacked the JDAM LAR (Launch Acceptability Region) information display in the cockpit. This meant that while manoeuvring, the crew of the B-1B might not have been aware that the aircraft had flown outside the LAR preventing JDAM bomb release.

While it would be foolish to pretend that the MK 82 iron bombs were precision delivered, the B-1B AN/APQ-164 SAR allowed the large bomber to deliver the weapons with a higher degree of accuracy than most other platforms in the inventory from the altitudes that they were delivered. The SAR also allowed the Lancer to penetrate heavy weather to deliver its ordnance. The Block D GPS upgrade allowed bombing on coordinates, which significantly increased bomb accuracy in comparison to the radar-offset bombing previously practised.

On a number of occasions, particularly 29 and 31 March, NATO tactical aircraft armed with laser guided bombs were forced to return to base without being able to drop their weapons due to cloud cover obscuring the target. The UK Parliamentary Report on Operation Allied Force states that this led to the request for the deployment of the USAF B-1B which would attempt to compensate by dropping huge numbers of unguided weapons. Indeed, the US DoD confirmed the B-1B Deployment on 29 March, along with the deployment of additional "all-weather" aircraft, assumed to be twelve additional F-117 Nighthawk strike aircraft, the deployment of which was confirmed on 1 April.

Ground crew remove the aircraft umbilical as a B-1B is prepared for a mission. Another pair of Lancers can been seen in the background. USAF

Around the same time Task Force Hawk was set up in Albania centred on 25 US Army AH-64 Apache attack helicopters and 18 MLRS (Multiple Launch Rocket Systems) which it was stated, were was to allow NATO a limited range strike capability into Kosovo from Albania, particularly when weather obscured targets from being struck from the air.

After initially mulling over flying the B-1B missions direct from Ellsworth AFB, South Dakota, to the Balkans, it was decided to base the bombers at RAF Fairford, in the UK to reduce the flight time from around 30-hours to around 7-hours. This would considerably ease the wear on aircraft and crew fatigue and, more importantly, would vastly reduce the need for in-flight refuelling, allowing tanker assets to be directed to other airborne platforms.

Initially four Block D and a single Block C B-1B were made available for Operation Allied Force and deployed to RAF Fairford from Ellsworth. The Block D UHF/VHF radios required temporary fixes for operation during the conflict; the Block D radio range being less than the Block C, although this had no negative impact on mission effectiveness. The mission planning software before the operation commenced was rated as unsatisfactory for combat operations, but this was waived to allow the bombers to participate in the campaign. Later additional aircraft were deployed to Fairford, with several more Block D aircraft flying operational sorties.

The Block D B-1B's that were eventually allocated for operations over the Balkans were put through a "crash" defensive systems upgrade program. This included installation of the Raytheon ALE-50 towed-radar-decoy system. Such was the haste of the upgrade that the aircraft that tested the new systems were the aircraft sent to Fairford. While the upgrade enhanced the bombers defence against threats, the new systems provided additional problems for ground crew. During the first ten or eleven days of operations, the B-1B force went through "a lot" of DAS (Defensive Aids System) line replaceable units. This problem alleviated when additional B-1B's were brought over to Fairford.

Above: A 77th BS B-1B gets airborne from RAF Fairford. USAF

Deployed aircraft were fitted with updated software as part of the Block cycle upgrade program before being dispatched to Fairford. The defensive mission data software allowed the B-1B Block D aircraft to more accurately identify and counter threats from hostile radar systems. The new systems were flight tested on 30 March 1999, just before the aircraft were cleared to participate in the campaign.

The USAF was able to deploy the small force of B-1B Lancers to RAF Fairford in just over four days; launching their first mission on the night of 1 April 1999 - some 14 hours after touching down at Fairford - when 2 Lancers from the 2nd AEG (Air Expeditionary Group) attacked what was claimed as a large staging area in Kosovo. Some accounts state that the First target to be attacked by B-1B's was the Novi Sud Oil Refinery located near Pancevo which lies to the North East of the Serbian Capital, Belgrade. However, USAF records, and statements from crew that flew the mission show quite clearly that the two B-1B's each did two bomb runs against mobile targets with about one minute between the respective weapons releases. Both targets were not only mobile, but had apparently moved from the original pre-mission target co-ordinates. The payload was apparently 168 x MK 82 500 lb. bombs, 84 carried by each of the two aircraft involved.

The ingress route for the Lancers took them across the Adriatic Sea, then apparently over Macedonia and Kosovo. On reaching the target the lead aircraft dropped its bombs, followed by the trail aircraft, Captained by 7th BW Vice Commander, Colonel Goodfellow, flying as a Flight Commander in the 77th BS, which, after releasing 32 x 500 lb. bombs over the first target, encountered a problem when one of the bomb bay doors would not close properly after bomb release. A weapon system malfunction prevented the aircraft releasing any further weapons over the first target. Goodfellow stated "I was able to fix the malfunction, but the bomb bay doors stayed open." The Lancer continued on mission to the second target, the aircraft dropping 40 x MK 82's.

Following bomb release by the trail aircraft egressing the second target area a SAM was observed, this, it was stated, was defeated by "Chaff, Electronic Countermeasures and manoeuvring". The Lancers countermeasures were the main defence against such weapons as no Lancer could realistically out-manoeuvre or outrun a missile on an accurate track that had not been decoyed by counter measures such as the AN/ALE-50 towed decoy which performed as planned on the mission, keeping the SAM well away from any of the Lancers. Another SAM was observed, this, it was stated, being defeated in the same manner as the first. The trail B-1B's woes were not over as the aircraft was apparently struck by Lighting on the return to Fairford, a portion of the horizontal stabilizer being lost, although the aircraft returned to make an safe landing at a rather murky Fairford after being in the air for around 14 hours according to USAF accounts. It has to be inferred that this aircraft brought back 12 of its 84 bombs as only 72 weapons were dropped, the other Lancer apparently dropping all 84 bombs.

Although, as recounted above, only five B-1B's were initially deployed, additional aircraft were made available as aircraft returned to the US for maintenance and inspection. The additional aircraft enabled the B-1B detachment to generate sortie rates that were typically two per-night on nights that missions were flown, although on at least three occasions four sorties per-night were flown. Carrying huge loads of MK 82 500-lb. bombs the B-1B's struck mainly area targets in Kosovo and Serbia. On some missions, such as the first, recounted above, aircraft struck two or more targets during the same sortie. During the first 30 days of B-1B operations, 1,500 MK 82 bombs were dropped on area targets.

Towards the end of the campaign the majority of the B-1B missions were flown in a "terminal guidance mode." This would involve a pair of B-1B's flying into the operational area, they then received targeting data from the CAOC (Combined Air Operations Centre) at Vicenza, Italy. Bomber target handoffs were enhanced through the use of a Boeing MSTS (Multi-Source Tactical System), which allowed digital information to be passed from the CAOC, or other sources, directly to the B-1B cockpit. This data included imagery, electronic order of battle and mission rehearsal data. Although enhancing the aircraft capabilities, this system was not crucial to the mission. One advantage of the system was to view the coordinates rather than just hear them over the radio. During the course of the campaign, B-1B's changed targets while en-route several times using the MSTS.

From 1 April until the end of the campaign, the B-1B detachment flew 74 operational sorties (apparently 81 sorties were launched, but only 74 dropped ordnance, the remaining seven either not releasing ordnance or being aborted for various reasons) with an average sortie length being claimed as around 7 to 8 hours. In excess of 5,000 MK 82 500-lb. bombs were released. USAF records show this to be in excess of 1260 tons, equating to around 20% of all ordnance delivered by all airborne platforms despite the fact that the B-1B detachment flew only 2% of sorties by NATO aircraft during the campaign. This impressive figure, it should be remembered, was offset by the fact that the ordnance was unguided, and although on most occasions it was dropped in the general area of the aim point, that aim point itself was area in nature. It would be prudent to conclude that most of the 5,000 or so weapons dropped by B-1B's failed to find a target other than that stated 'area'. In many cases, such as at air bases, vast cratering was designed to cause maximum disruption to operations.

What the campaign showed was that the B-1B was an effective bomb truck, hauling loads of 42,000 lb. of conventional bombs to area targets.

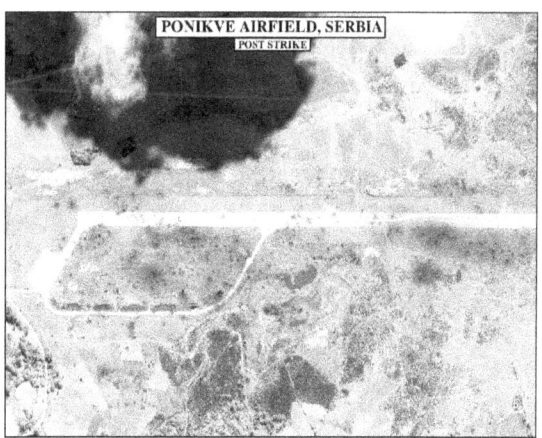

The runway at Ponikve airfield shows extensive cratering following strategic bomber strikes. NATO

Top: The long snout of a B-1B stands over a row of MK 82 500-lb. bombs waiting to be loaded onto the aircraft at Fairford in May 1999. Above: A B-1B is partially obscured by its own artificial heat haze caused by the massive thrust of its four afterburning turbofan engines as it leaves Fairford on a bombing mission in May 1999. USAF

A B-1B Lancer touches down at the end of a 7-hour bombing mission against targets in the Balkans. USAF

While on average there was less than half the numbers of B-1B's at Fairford than there were B-52H's, the B-1B detachment dropped 45% of all ordnance delivered from Fairford. During the campaign the B-1B's and B-52H detachments at Fairford delivered 11,650 weapons averaging around 45 per sortie. The 7.3 million pounds of ordnance delivered cost around $24 million. These figures excluded the AGM-86 CALCM, around 60 of which had been launched by 16 April, which when acquisition cost of the AGM-86B and the conversion cost to AGM-86C are taken into account, cost around $1.2 million per missile.

When the ceasefire came into effect on 9 June 1999, the Lancers remained at Fairford for a further two weeks before returning home to Elssworth AFB, South Dakota on 23 June.

While the NATO air campaign had angered Russia, Russian diplomatic moves assisted in bringing the conflict to an end. Ironically, the campaign ended with a NATO embarrassment as a Russian armoured column raced through Bosnia to seize Pristina airfield before NATO troops could reach it from Macedonia. Only western diplomatic pressure on countries wishing western aid prevented the Russians from airlifting in large reinforcements. However, the Russian point had been made, and NATO humbled before a watching world.

During the campaign, NATO flew 38,000 sorties over the course of 78 days of operations. Of this total, over 15,000 sorties were flown by non-US NATO partners with the remainder flown by the US. Compared to the 1991 Persian Gulf War, in which coalition forces flew 40,000 strike sorties in 30 days, in Allied Force NATO aircrews flew only 9,000 strike sorties in 78 days. There were 57 days of actual air strikes. Ordnance was dropped on around 7,600 fixed target aim points (USAF records show this to be 421 fixed targets, the figure of 7,600 being made up of multiple aim points on a single target. Statistically analysis showed that the USAF considered that only 35% of these fixed targets were destroyed. In addition there were over 3,400 flex target aim points. Overall, 70 percent of weapons released during those 9,000 sorties were precision-guided munitions. The B-1B and B-52H heavy bombers dropped the bulk of the non-precision guided ordnance.

A trio of B-52H bombers taxi at Fairford prior to a mission over the Balkans. USAF

It is often stated that fifteen B-1B and B-52H's flew operations from Fairford. However, this was an average strength with additional bombers of both types rotating through Fairford from the US and no less than three B-52H's arriving at Fairford from Diego Garcia in the Indian Ocean.

During the course of the campaign NATO destroyed or severely damaged 11 rail bridges, 34 road bridges, a claimed 57% of petroleum reserves, all Federal Republic of Yugoslavia oil refineries, 14 command posts and ten airfields

While Operation Allied Force was a success in that NATO was finally able to enter its forces into Kosovo unmolested, it failed in its military objective of crippling the Serbian military. While NATO was reasonably successful in hitting large fixed targets such as buildings or air bases, it failed to make much of an impact on its attacks on Serbian ground forces.

Like most operators of the various assets the bombers force reported much success against fielded forces during the campaign, however, post war analysis showed beyond doubt that NATO's claims were grossly exaggerated about Serbian military equipment destroyed. In many cases large numbers of bombs would be dropped with no effect against fielded forces.

In real-terms NATO operating restrictions about aircraft attacking fielded forces was almost like modern health and safety gone mad. In order to be reasonably sure of zero casualties on each mission the effectiveness of the attacking force was severely compromised, in some cases to the extent that the mission would have been as well not being flown. Combined with. In particular, the altitude restrictions imposed on most NATO aircraft, in order to reduce vulnerability to air defences, was unsuitable for attacking fielded forces. This, combined with unfavourable weather on a number of days massively reduced the potential for NATO air power to have the desired impact on ground forces.

Multiple craters can be seen on Obrva airfield following attacks be NATO aircraft. NATO

A B-52H commences its take-off run at Fairford at the start of a mission against Serbian targets on the penultimate day of the campaign, 8 June 1999. USAF

The geography of Kosovo was a world apart from the flat open desert terrain of Kuwait and Iraq, allowing the Serb forces to use a combination of cover and tactics which included operating in smaller tactical units to avoid the worst of NATO's air campaign. Much of NATO's claims were vastly overstated for propaganda reasons and many targets, which were hit, were simply crudely prepared mock-up targets, which were used to good effect by the Serbs, both among fielded forces and at fixed sites such as air bases. Post war many of these mock-ups, which included aircraft, canvas tanks and SAM sites were revealed.

The US after action reports claimed that one reason there was a lack of evidence of tactical targets destroyed in Kosovo was because on site inspections were not conducted in some areas until one month after the conflict ended, during which time the Serbs may have removed damaged or destroyed vehicles. However, this is not a possibility as NATO was the military force present in Kosovo from 10 June, not the Serbs. There was no possibility for the Serbs to remove damaged or destroyed military equipment after NATO's entry into the province. Once the smoke screens had cleared, the evidence available was irrefutable that NATO was much less successful than it claimed in striking tactical targets in Kosovo.

While NATO claims to have defeated the Serbian military, what is clear is that an organised military force withdrew from Kosovo and not a disorganised rabble, which would be expected from a defeated army. What finally forced the Serbs to agree to NATO's demands was the fact that the countries infrastructure was being destroyed. While Serbia had not suffered a massive military defeat, economically it could not sustain the war as the country was pushed towards financial ruin.

Operation Allied Force showed that the B-1B was a competent conventional bomber capable of hauling huge tonnage of weapons to distant targets. This pair of Lancers sits alongside a row of MK 82 500-lb. bombs, the only munitions expended by the B-1B during the campaign. USAF

It is easy to write about conflict as though it were only machines that were involved. The absence of a human cost for NATO during the campaign makes it far too easy to overlook the human cost. It would be pertinent, therefore to detail some of the more controversial incidents of the campaign. In point of fact, it would be less than prudent not to do so.

The following is a chronology of major incidents during the 1999 campaign:

24 March: The NATO air offensive against Serbia and Kosovo commenced.

26 March: The first surge of refugees crossed from Kosovo into Albania.

27 March: The first NATO combat aircraft loss occurred when a USAF Lockheed Martin F-117A Nighthawk was shot down by a Serbian SAM near Belgrade. The pilot ejected from the stricken aircraft and was recovered.

31 March: In the only known ground incident between NATO and Serbian forces, three US soldiers were captured by Serb forces on the Macedonian/Kosovo border.

5 April: A bomb dropped from a NATO aircraft hits a residential area in Aleksinac in southern Serbia

9 April: A number of houses are destroyed or damaged in Pristina, Kosovo with an undisclosed number of casualties. A telephone exchange nearby was the target.

12 April: During an attack on a target on a rail bridge at Grdelicka Klisura in southern Serbia a USAF aircraft hit a civilian passenger train with two missiles killing a large number of passengers.

13 April: As KLA forces continued to cross into Kosovo from bases in Albania, Serb forces launched a cross border raid in northern Albania.

14 April: NATO aircraft bomb Kosovo civilian refugee columns killing a large number of civilians and injuring many more.

21 April: NATO bombed the HQ of the Federal Republic of Yugoslavia government.

23 April: NATO aircraft bombed the Serbian State Television, which was protected under the Geneva Convention.

28 April: The Yugoslav government accepts the presence of an international military force in Kosovo, but this is rejected by NATO, which wanted, or needed, a NATO operation in Kosovo.

28 April: NATO bombed a residential area in the village of Surdulica, 150 miles south of Belgrade, killing around 20 civilians. NATO stated that the aim point was an army barracks in the area. Such attacks in civilian areas were extremely questionable, as military barracks would have been evacuated in the first days of the war, or indeed the lead up to hostilities, leaving empty buildings of no tactical or strategic value

May: The G8 agreed on a basis for a peace plan, which called for the return of all refugees and the deployment into Kosovo of an international "security" force. However, the sticking point with this remained NATO's desire to see a NATO force deployed into Kosovo rather than a United Nations force. The problem with this was that NATO was to all intents and purposes at war with Yugoslavia, therefore, the Serbs saw a NATO deployment into Kosovo as an occupation force.

1 May: NATO aircraft bombed a bridge at Luzane near Pristina in Kosovo striking a civilian bus and killing a stated 47 passengers.

5 May: A US Army Boeing AH-64A Apache attack helicopter crashed in Albania killing both crew. The Apaches were part of a NATO build-up of forces in Albania, which included attack helicopters, armour and artillery including MLRS (Multiple Launch Rocket Systems).

7 May: A NATO aircraft dropped a cluster bomb in central Nis in southeast Serbia killing, it was reported, around 15 civilians and injuring around 70 more.

8 May: A B-2A bombed the Chinese Embassy in Belgrade killing three Chinese civilians. NATO described the incident as a mistake; however, China was infuriated as the Embassy building was proven to be the target, although the US later claimed it thought the building was used by the Serbs. There have been a number of theories regarding this incident, with "faulty information: being the official US story. This would amount to a major intelligence failure as the average tourist could, without difficulty, pinpoint the Chinese Embassy on a tourist map of Belgrade.

10 May: Yugoslavia took its case to the UN International Court of Justice to try and get an order for NATO to stop its bombing campaign. However, the Court ruled that it lacked the jurisdiction over such a case.

13/14 May: NATO aircraft bomb Korisa, a village in southern Kosovo, killing an estimated 79 civilians and wounding a further 58 according to various reports.

20 May: Around one O'clock in the morning a hospital in Belgrade was apparently struck by a NATO bomb or missile, which NATO claimed was aimed at a military barracks.

21 May: Russia reported that its talks with NATO were deadlocked as NATO stuck to its demands for the agreement to allow NATO forces to occupy Kosovo.

22 May: NATO aircraft bombed positions held by the KLA at Kosare, killing a number of KLA fighters.

23 May: As Serbia attempted to destroy KLA supply lines on the Albanian border, Albanian and Serb forces clashed.

29 May: The Yugoslav government announced that it had accepted the G8 proposals for a peace deal.

30 May: NATO aircraft bombed a road bridge at Varvarin during a daylight attack. A number of civilians using the bridge were reported killed.

31 May: As NATO bombing continued, a Sanatorium at Surdulica in southern Serbia was struck. On the same day a four story-housing block was struck by NATO bombs during an attack on the town of Novi Pazar. NATO confirmed that at least one bomb had struck a residential area.

1 June: The Yugoslav government handed a letter to the German government stating that it "has accepted G8 principles"

9 June: Following days of talks, NATO and Yugoslav military leaders signed the military technical agreement, which would see Serb forces withdrawn from Kosovo and NATO forces move into the province. One of the major sticking points had been NATO's insistence that Serb forces begin its withdrawal while air strikes were on going. This was flatly rejected by Belgrade as it would have exposed Serb forces to air attack while being out in the open.

10 June: NATO officially suspended air strikes.

Appendices

Appendix I

Serial Numbers of B-52H, and B-1B bombers involved in Operation Allied Force

2nd Expeditionary Air Group

B-52H - 2nd Bomb Wing Barksdale AFB, Louisiana
(20th, 11th and 96th Bomb Squadrons)

60-0010
60-0011
60-0014
60-0016
60-0020
60-0022
60-0037
60-0043
60-0046
60-0049
60-0052
60-0059
60-0062
61-0002
61-0011
61-0016
61-0020
61-0023
61-0031
60-0039

5th Bomb Wing, Minot AFB, North Dakota (Aircraft from 23rd Bomb Squadron)

60-0009
60-0018
60-0033
60-0044
60-0051

B-1B - 28th Bomb Wing, Ellsworth AFB, South Dakota. (Aircraft from 77th and 37th Bomb Squadrons) 16th AEW

85-0073
85-0074
85-0075
85-0083
85-0091
85-0097
86-0102
86-0104
86-0129

Appendix II

509th BW

B-2A

Unfortunately there is no official published list of B-2A's that took part in operations over the Balkans. It is assumed that at least eight of the average of nine operationally available B-2A's took part in bombing missions.

Serial numbers of the 21 B-2A's delivered are as follows:

82-1066 to 82-1071, 88-328 to 88-332, 89-172 to 89-129, 90-040 to 90-041, 92-700, 93-1085 to 93-1088 Note: Not all B-2A's were in service at the time; the last B-2A being delivered to the USAF in 2000

Appendix III

Weapons employed

B-52
AGM-86C Block 1 CALCM
AGM-142 Have Nap
MK 82 500 lb. Bomb
GBU LGB

B-1B
MK 82 500 lb. bomb

B-2A
GBU 31 JDAM
GBU 37 4,700 lb. Class guided bomb

Glossary

AAA	Anti-Aircraft Artillery
ACC	Air Combat Command
ACM	Advanced Cruise Missile
AEW	Airborne Early Warning
AFB	Air Force Base
AFFTC	Air Force Flight Test Centre
AGM	Air to Ground Missile
ALBM	Air Launched Ballistic Missile
ALCM	Air Launched Cruise Missile
AMC	Air Mobility Command
AMRAAM	Advanced Medium Range Air to Air Missile
ATB	Advanced Tactical Bomber
AWACS	Airborne Warning and Control System
B	Bomber
BDA	Bomb Damage Assessment
BS	Bomb Squadron
BW	Bomb Wing
CALCM	Conventional Air Launched Cruise Missile
CBU	Cluster Bomb Unit
CENTCOM	Central Command
CEP	Circular Error of Probability
CMUP	Conventional Munitions Upgrade Program
CONUS	Continental United States
DoD	Department of Defence
E	Electronic
EA	Electronic Attack
ECM	Electronic Counter Measures
EMD	Engineering Manufacturing Development
EU	European Union
F	Fighter
F/A	Fighter/Attack
FLIR	Forward Looking Infrared
FY	Fiscal Year
GATS	GPS Aided Targeting System
GBU	Guided Bomb Unit
GPS	Global Positioning System
GR	Ground attack Reconnaissance
HARM	High Speed Anti-Radiation Missile
HMS	Her Majesty's Ship
HQ	Headquarters
HSAB	Heavy Stores Adaptor Beam
INS	Inertial Navigation System
IOC	Initial Operational Capability
IR	Infrared
JASSM	Joint Air to Surface Stand-off Missile
JDAM	Joint Direct Attack Munitions
JSOW	Joint Stand-Off Weapon
JSTARS	Joint Surveillance Target Attack Radar System
KC	Tanker Transport
LDGP	Low Drag General Purpose
LGB	Laser Guided Bomb
LLLTV	Low Light Level Television
LRIP	Low Rate Initial Production
MBDA	Matra British Aerospace Dynamics Alenia
MOD	Ministry Of Defence
NASA	National Aeronautics and Space Administration
NATO	North Atlantic Treaty Organisation
NVG	Night Vision Goggles
SAC	Strategic Air Command
SACEUR	Supreme Allied Commander Europe
SAM	Surface to Air Missile
SAR	Synthetic Aperture Radar
SIGINT	Signals Intelligence
SRAM	Short Range Attack Missile
SSN	Nuclear powered attack Submarine
TAC	Tactical Air Command
TLAM	Tomahawk Land Attack Missile
TV	Television
UAV	Uninhabited Air Vehicle
UK	United Kingdom
UN	United Nations
US	United States
USA	United States of America
USAF	United States Air Force
USMC	United States Marine Corp
USN	United States Navy

www.ingramcontent.com/pod-product-compliance
Lightning Source LLC
Chambersburg PA
CBHW081329190426
43193CB00044B/2899